For Sophie, above all.

Éditions Mille et une vies
56230 Questembert – France
www.editions1001vies.fr

ISBN : 979-10-96138-49-4

Olivier Cousin

DM QUIZ

250 questions about Depeche Mode
for Devotees

LES ÉDITIONS
MILLE ET UNE VIES

Table of contents

Introduction

1980-2025: Forty-five years... Just what we needed for a little quiz! So much has happened in Depeche Mode's career, big and small, that you're bound to have questions about the band if you like them or if you're just a bit curious.

And these questions can also be asked for fun, whether you're a Devotee – the nickname given to Depeche Mode fans since the 1993 "Devotional Tour" – from the very beginning, or a fan wanting to find out more about this cult band. These pages take a closer look at the history of a band that, album after album since 1989, has filled stadiums the world over. Depeche Mode has been around since 1980, with a striking evolution: from naive synth pop to electro rock reviving the roots of the blues, with an uncompromising search for original sounds and, despite everything, hits throughout its career, some of which are downright timeless.

Forty-five years! Without even a period of separation, the longest break between albums having been six years. Depeche Mode never announced that they were stopping, unlike many bands who, like them, started out at the dawn of the 1980s. Today few bands from the same movement are continuing a career that began so long ago: with DM (as they'll often be called below), U2, Simple Minds and a handful of others which could be counted on the fingers of both our hands.

With four members at the start (1980-1981), then three (1982), then four again (1982-1995), then three again (1995-2022), and finally two today, Depeche Mode has managed to build a solid career, which in its early days was met with disdain by a large part of the music world, and which today is experiencing a quasi-deification that sometimes embarrasses its members. But it's also a career that has gone through some – sometimes very – critical phases, which you can (re)discover in the following pages. Why and how did Depeche Mode become a cult band, the ultimate cult electro-rock band?

From Basildon's patronage halls in Essex and the more or less glamorous pubs of East London to concert halls all over the world, and then to the great stadiums of the five continents, Depeche Mode has come to give the full measure of its musical and lyrical richness on stage. Which is a huge paradox for a synthetic music group: three guys frozen behind keyboards with a singer, the only frontman, using his sexy hips to move with the crowd. They had to find strategies and set designs to create dynamic, perhaps minimalist, but well-oiled gigs, capable of captivating crowds of fans. And, because let's face it, Depeche Mode are the band of paradoxes, they've succeeded! Communication with the audience is almost always total ("black celebration" or not), whereas the band communicates very little: in Depeche Mode no one on stage tells their life stories or funny anecdotes between songs... Yet their fan base, their community of countless loyal fans, remains one of the most active and grateful on the rock circuit.

This quiz is for them... Now it's up to them!

This serious yet entertaining quiz contains 250 multiple-choice questions in five categories:
- the first is entitled "DM In person" and focuses on the members of Depeche Mode, their history, and the ups and downs of the life of a band that has become a star;
- Part two, "DM On records", reviews the records, recordings, titles, songs – in other words, the work that has enabled DM to become and remain a cult band year after year;
- Part three, "DM Visual", looks at the band's album covers and videos, as well as magazine covers, books, advertising and promotional appearances involving DM and its members;
- Part four, "DM Live", takes us back to the band's tours and concerts;
- Finally, Part five, "DM & Co.", looks at DM's tributes, influences, covers, collaborations and the solo work of the group's members.

A final table allows those who wish to do so to visualise clearly their achievements and assess their degree of Devotee attitude... And there are sure to be some surprises!

The answers, placed at the end of each sub-section, expand on some of the information that gives the book an "encyclopaedic" aspect to the group's history and anecdotes, in addition to the fun aspect that will no doubt come first for many readers.

Part I

DM IN PERSON

01 *The founding members of Depeche Mode grew up in* ***Basildon****, a modern, soulless town – it is often said – on the outskirts of London, about thirty kilometres from the centre. Where is exactly Basildon?*

A) North of London ☐
B) South of London ☐
C) East of London ☐
D) West of London ☐

02 *The Basildon Four, they are sometimes called. Yet none of the original members were born in Basildon. So, who was* ***really born*** *where?*

A) Vince Clarke	a) Epping (in Essex)
B) Martin Gore	b) Dagenham (East London)
C) Dave Gahan	c) South Woodford (East London)
D) Andrew Fletcher	d) Nottingham

03 *Put in chronological order the* ***three bands*** *formed by the members (not necessarily all together) before they founded Depeche Mode:*

A) Composition of Sound / No Romance in China / The French Look ☐
B) No Romance in China / The French Look / Composition of Sound ☐
C) No Romance in China / Composition of Sound / The French Look ☐

04 *What **instrument** did Andy Fletcher originally play in Composition of Sound, the first band he joined with Vince Clarke and Martin Gore?*

A) guitar ☐
B) bass ☐
C) drums ☐
D) keyboards ☐

05 *According to the testimony of Vince Clarke himself, in what **strange circumstances** did he first meet Martin Gore in Basildon when they were both aged around 15-16?*

A) Vince was playing with Andy in the church hall and Martin attended their concert ☐
B) Vince was walking past Martin's house and Martin was sitting drunk in the bushes ☐
C) at a school cricket match where they were on opposing teams ☐
D) at a meeting of the Boys' Brigade of St Paul's Methodist Church in Basildon ☐

06 *Which of these four bands did Martin Gore never play in?*

A) The French Look ☐
B) Composition of Sound ☐
C) Daphne & the Tenderspots ☐
D) Norman & the Worms ☐

07 *In the Spring of 1980, when he impressed Vince Clarke, then a member of Composition of Sound, what* ***song*** *was Dave Gahan singing?*

A) Iggy Pop's 'Lust for Life' ☐
B) David Bowie's 'Heroes' ☐
C) Roxy Music's 'Angel Eyes' ☐
D) Kraftwerk's 'The Model' ☐

08 *When Martin Gore was a teenager, which British artist was he enough of a fan of to join his* ***official fan club****?*

A) David Bowie ☐
B) Bryan Ferry ☐
C) Gary Glitter ☐
D) Marc Bolan ☐

09 *The group has only had five official members. Give each of them their* ***date of birth****:*

A) Vince Clarke	a) 9 May 1962
B) Andrew Fletcher	b) 23 July 1961
C) Dave Gahan	c) 1 June 1959
D) Martin Lee Gore	d) 8 July 1961
E) Alan Wilder	e) 3 July 1960

10 *Who came up with the* ***French-sounding name*** *Depeche Mode to replace Composition of Sound – which probably sounded too much like an experimental band?*

A) Martin Gore ☐
B) Vince Clarke ☐
C) Andy Fletcher ☐
D) Dave Gahan ☐

11 *Back in the days of Composition of Sound and the early days of DM, at which band member's house did they* ***rehearse****?*

A) Martin Gore's ☐
B) Vince Clarke's ☐
C) Andy Fletcher's ☐
D) Dave Gahan's ☐

12 *When they released their first album on 5 October 1981, the four members of Depeche Mode were still* ***modest employees****. Who was doing what?*

A) Dave Gahan	a) Nat West bank clerk
B) Vince Clarke	b) apprentice stock boy
C) Martin Gore	c) Sun Life insurance company employee
D) Andy Fletcher	d) worker in a dairy factory

13 *When he was at* ***secondary school****, in which subject was Martin Gore the best?*

A) History ☐
B) Languages ☐
C) Maths ☐
D) Sports ☐

14 *How did Vince Clarke describe the music he produced on* **Speak & Spell***, with its rather primitive lyrics and repetitive, jerky yet melodic sounds?*

A) Electro pop ☐
B) Techno pop ☐
C) Ultra pop ☐
D) Synth pop ☐

15 *Before applying to play with DM, in which British* ***music weekly*** *did Alan Wilder read the band's advert looking for a new synth player in early 1982?*

A) *Sounds* ☐
B) *NME* ☐
C) *Melody Makers* ☐
D) *Record Mirror* ☐

16 *Struggling to make ends meet before joining DM in 1982, Alan Wilder was often short of cash. He was even arrested for* ***shoplifting*** *in 1981. What did he steal?*

A) an LP ☐
D) some beer ☐
C) a 7" single ☐
D) some chicken ☐

17 *Rank the five members of DM* ***from smallest to tallest****:*

A) Vince Clarke, Martin Gore, Dave Gahan, Alan Wilder, Andy Fletcher ☐
B) Alan Wilder, Vince Clarke, Martin Gore, Dave Gahan, Andy Fletcher ☐
C) Martin Gore, Vince Clarke, Alan Wilder, Dave Gahan, Andy Fletcher ☐

18 *What was the name of the* ***sound engineer*** *who set up Blackwing Studios in London, where DM recorded all his songs until 1983?*

A) Gareth Jones ☐
D) Flood ☐
C) Eric Radcliffe ☐

19 *Do you know the name of Martin Gore's* ***first fiancée****, who followed the band from the start?*

A) Deb Danahay ☐
B) Joanne Fox ☐
C) Anne Swindell ☐

20 *When he was just 23, following the mixing of the album* Construction Time Again *at Berlin's Hansa studio in July 1983, Martin Gore decided to share a flat there with his* ***German girlfriend****, called:*

A) Erna ☐
B) Christina ☐
C) Paula ☐
D) Eva ☐

21 *In what year did Dave Gahan dye his hair* ***platinum blonde****, leaving Alan Wilder as the only non-blond member of the band for a few months?*

A) 1983 ☐
B) 1985 ☐
C) 1987 ☐
D) 1988 ☐

22 *Which members of the group are avowed **vegetarians**?*

A) Dave Gahan ☐
B) Martin Gore ☐
C) Andy Fletcher ☐
D) Alan Wilder ☐

23 *Between the end of 1983 and 1984, Dave Gahan took lessons from a world-renowned **vocal coach** called:*

A) Mona van Spit ☐
B) Tona de Brett ☐
C) Phila de Jong ☐

24 *Andy Fletcher has a reputation for playing one **game** very well. Which game is it?*

A) billiards ☐
B) chess ☐
C) darts ☐
D) poker ☐

25 *In what year did Andy Fletcher marry his long-time girlfriend* ***Gráinne Mullan****?*

A) 1990 ☐
B) 1991 ☐
C) 1992 ☐
D) 1993 ☐

26 *It's common knowledge among fans – who would even swear they've seen him taste them on stage – that Andy Fletcher's* ***favourite fruit*** *is:*

A) apples ☐
B) oranges ☐
C) pineapples ☐
D) bananas ☐

27 *What was Dave Gahan's unofficial* ***pet nickname*** *in the 90s?*

A) the Feline ☐
B) the Cat ☐
C) the Snake ☐
D) the Jaguar ☐

28 *By the way, what is Dave Gahan's* ***birth name****?*

A) Prescott ☐
B) Calldicott ☐
C) Phillpott ☐
D) Callcott ☐

29 *Dave Gahan's* ***largest tattoo*** *covers his upper back, from shoulder blade to shoulder blade, and took over ten hours to complete in 1993. What does it represent?*

A) a woman with her arms outstretched and her hands open ☐
B) the spread wings of a demon ☐
C) symmetrical bird wings ☐

30 *In what part of London was Martin Gore's small studio located when he was still* ***living in London****?*

A) Camden ☐
B) Maida Vale ☐
C) Notting Hill ☐
D) Chelsea ☐

31 *Alan Wilder probably had the fright of his life on 1 September 1994, as he drove his* ***Mercedes 300SL*** *convertible through the Scottish glens, not far from Lochearnhead. Why?*

A) he fell into a ravine and owed his survival only to a group of walkers ☐
B) while he was driving, an eagle attacked him, wounding him in the head ☐
C) his car was almost hit by an RAF fighter plane ☐
D) he hit a couple of deer, which caused him to roll over ☐

32 *Do you know if Alan Wilder has any* ***children****?*

A) no, he doesn't ☐
B) yes, 1 girl and 1 boy ☐
C) yes, 2 girls and 1 boy ☐
D) yes, 1 boy ☐

33 *Who is* ***Jonathan Kessler*** *to the band?*

A) no one in particular ☐
B) their fiercest critic ☐
C) their clothing consultant ☐
D) their long-time manager ☐

34 *What was the name of the **restaurant** Andy Fletcher bought in London in 1993?*

A) Burgundy Restaurant and Bar ☐
B) Normandy Restaurant and Bar ☐
C) Biarritz Restaurant and Bar ☐
D) Gascogne Restaurant and Bar ☐

35 *What do you think Dave Gahan nicknamed "the **Purple Palace**" in the 90s?*

A) his own house in Hollywood ☐
B) the London offices of Mute Records ☐
C) the rehab centre imposed on him by the Californian courts ☐

36 *When did Alan Wilder announce in an **official statement** that he was quitting Depeche Mode?*

A) 1 January 1995 ☐
B) 1 April 1995 ☐
C) 1 June 1995 ☐
D) 1 September 1995 ☐

37 *In May 1996, Dave Gahan took a second* ***overdose****, this one so serious that his heart stopped beating for almost two minutes. In which Los Angeles hotel did this tragedy take place?*

A) the Beverly Hills Hotel ☐
B) the Sofitel Los Angeles ☐
C) the Sunset Marquis Hotel ☐
D) the Fairmont Miramar Hotel ☐

38 *From 2002 Andy Fletcher was the boss of a small* ***music label****, under the aegis of Mute, which was then mothballed in 2006. What was its name?*

A) Tequila Music ☐
B) Daikiri Records ☐
C) Ananas Label ☐
D) Toast Hawaii ☐

39 *During the 2000s, Andy Fletcher sometimes did* ***DJ sets*** *in London. What name did he go under?*

A) Andy F ☐
B) DJ F ☐
C) Client F ☐
D) Fletch ☐

40 *None of the five historic members of the group is an only child. But one of them is an elder son with **only sisters**. Who is concerned?*

A) Vince ☐
B) Andy ☐
C) Dave ☐
D) Martin ☐
E) Alan ☐

41 *At the end of 1985, Martin Gore needed a break after a period of disappointment and annoyance: the demos he had prepared for the forthcoming album had not been very well received by the people around Mute to whom Daniel Miller had played them. So, what did he do in secret to take a **step back**?*

A) he went off with his German girlfriend to an almost deserted island in the Baltic Sea ☐
B) he locked himself in his Berlin flat and turned off the phone ☐
C) he went off alone to compose new demos in the south of France ☐
D) he retired to the family farm of his college pen pal in Germany ☐

42 *Which band member didn't* ***DJ****?*

A) V. Clarke ☐
B) A. Fletcher ☐
C) D. Gahan ☐
D) M. Gore ☐
E) A. Wilder ☐

43 *Martin Gore has married twice. What are the names of his successive* ***wives****?*

A) Kerrilee Barki, then Marianne Robert ☐
B) Suzanne Boisvert, then Kerrilee Kaski ☐
C) Marianne Robert, then Kerrilee Barki ☐
D) Kerrilee Kask, then Suzanne Boisvert ☐

44 *What are the first names, in chronological order, of the three* ***women*** *married to Dave Gahan?*

A) Joanne / Jennifer / Teresa ☐
B) Joanne / Teresa / Jennifer ☐
C) Teresa / Jennifer / Joanne ☐

45 *In which Rhode Island* ***seaside town*** *has Dave Gahan owned a second home since 2005?*

A) Long Beach ☐
B) Coney Island ☐
C) Montauk ☐
D) Amityville ☐

46 *List* ***Martin Gore's children****, which are ranked here in alphabetical order, from youngest to oldest: Ava Lee, Calo Leon, Johnnie Lee, Mazzy Lee, Viva Lee.*

A) Ava Lee, Calo Leon, Mazzy Lee, Johnnie Lee, Viva Lee ☐
B) Calo Leon, Johnnie Lee, Ava Lee, Viva Lee, Mazzy Lee ☐
C) Viva Lee, Ava Lee, Calo Leon, Johnnie Lee, Mazzy Lee ☐

47 *Martin Gore can boast of having won a highly prestigious songwriting award in the UK for his talents as a composer and lyricist: the* ***Ivor Novello Award*** *from the British Academy of Songwriters, Composers and Authors for International Achievement. What year did he win it?*

A) 1989 ☐
B) 1999 ☐
C) 2009 ☐
D) 2019 ☐

48 *What does Martin Gore call his "**Electric Ladyboy**"?*

A) the computer where he keeps all his compositions ☐
B) the rare guitar he dreams of owning one day ☐
C) his personal recording studio ☐
D) his favourite vintage Korg synth ☐

49 *In what year was Depeche Mode elected to join the **Rock and Roll Hall of Fame**?*

A) 2015 ☐
B) 2018 ☐
C) 2020 ☐
D) 2022 ☐

50 *What is **Andy Fletcher's date of death**?*

A) 16 May 2022 ☐
B) 26 May 2022 ☐
C) 6 June 2022 ☐
D) 16 June 2022 ☐

1. C

Basildon is situated to the east of London.

2. A-c / B-b / C-a / D-d.

3. B

No Romance in China: Vince Clarke and Andy Fletcher / The French Look: Martin Gore and a singer called Rob Marlow, another friend from Basildon / Composition of Sound: V. Clarke, A. Fletcher, with the addition of M. Gore (who still played in The French Look) and then D. Gahan in 1980.

4. B

A. Fletcher played bass at the start of Composition of Sound, and before that in No Romance in China with V. Clarke.

5. B

Testimony of Vince Clarke to Jonathan Miller reported in *Stripped: Depeche Mode* (p. 11).

6. C

Daphne & The Tenderspots was a London band in which Alan Wilder played between two other bands he was involved with, Dragons (in Bristol) and then Real To Real. Norman & The Worms was the duo made up of Martin Gore and guitarist Phil Burdett, who already had a version of 'See You' in their repertoire in 1979...

7. B

'Heroes' by David Bowie. As fate would have it, the band started playing this song live on the "Global Spirit Tour" in 2017, a year after Bowie's death. It has often been said that the anecdote of Gahan singing 'Heroes' took place in a studio where the others would have heard it, unexpectedly, in another room of the studio, but it actually happened in a college in Basildon, Woodlands School, on a Wednesday night when the bands Composition of Sound and The French Look were rehearsing in two different rooms before a gig in the foyer (as Jonathan Miller accurately explains in *Stripped: Depeche Mode*, p. 29). Gahan was accompanying his pal Paul Redmond, keyboardist in The French Look, a band to whom Gahan was lending a hand; and, during a break, Vince Clarke heard The French Look playing Bowie in another room. He thought the rendition of 'Heroes' was very good and suggested to Martin and Andy that he might be a good singer for them. Vince Clarke accurately recounts that it was a few days later that they decided to audition Dave, asking him to sing two songs written by Clarke and one Roxy Music song, which he performed better than the other two. Vince makes no secret of the fact that Dave Gahan was popular and hipper than the other three, which played a part in their decision to retain him as frontman.

8. C

Is there a nod to this devotion to the seventies glam rock star in the name of one of the remixes on the B-side of the 12" of 'Never Let Me Down Again' (reference 12 BONG 14): the "Glitter Mix" of 'Pleasure, Little Treasure'?

9. A-e / B-d / C-a / D-b / E-c

10. D

Dave Gahan, more of a fashion victim than most (in terms of looks, he was considered one of Basildon's New Romantics) and an apprentice in the clothing shop decorating branch, was familiar with fashion magazines and in particular the French magazine – and therefore with two accents – *Dépêche Mode* (in the sense of "news of/about fashion") whose name meant something like hurried/fast fashion to him. The name of the band didn't change until the second half of 1980, when they played five shows at the Crocs Glamour Club in Rayleigh from 16 August 1980 (as part of Futurist Nights), and in London at the Bridgehouse in Canning Town on 24 September 1980 under the name Composition of Sound. The first concert under the name Depeche Mode took place on 29 October 1980 in a London club (Ronnie Scott's Jazz Club in Soho).

11. B

The rehearsals took place in the garage on the ground floor of the house of Vince Clarke's mother, Mrs Rose Martin, in the Mynchens area of Basildon.

12. A-b / B-d / C-a / D-c.

13. B

Languages (German and French).

14. C

Ultra Pop. Who knows if the band remembered this U.P. when it came to finding a title for the 1997 album, *Ultra*...

15. C

Melody Makers. Ironically – or not – it was also in this magazine that Vince Clarke would, a few years later, place the same kind of ad to find the singer he was looking for for the duo that was to become Erasure. Although Alan was recruited as a touring musician in early 1982, he wasn't officially a member of the band until October 1982, as the Depeche Mode Official Information Service newsletter for that month shows. Indeed, DM were keen to prove that it was the three of them who had changed their musical direction after Vince Clarke's departure, without the help of a newcomer. And in October, once the album *A Broken Frame* (recorded without the participation of Alan, though he had already been playing some tracks on stage for several months) was well underway, the trio decided to integrate it completely.

16. D

Chicken.

17. A

Vince Clarke (1.70 m), Martin Gore (1.74 m), Dave Gahan (1.78 m), Alan Wilder (1.80 m), Andy Fletcher (1.92 m). The heights given here may be wrong to within a few centimetres, as the figures may differ from one source to another.

18. C

This is Eric from the title of the Yazoo album *Upstairs at Eric's* (1982), a reference to the floor of Blackwing, the former small church where Radcliffe had his quarters. After Yazoo, he took part in Vince Clarke's The Assembly project. He and Clarke also set up Reset Records (1983-1987), a small label that released four singles by Robert Marlow, another long-time Basildonian.

19. C

Anne Swindell. She plays the daughter that D. Gahan is looking for in the video for 'See You'. At the same time, Deb Danahay and Joanne Fox were the girlfriends of Vince Clarke and Dave Gahan respectively and looked after the band's fan club.

20. B

Christina Friederich. In the Charlottenburg district of Berlin.

21. B

1985. By September 1983, D. Gahan already had blond locks, as can be seen in the videos for 'Love, in Itself' and 'People Are People'; and in early 1984, he also sported a mullet, which can be seen in 'Master and Servant'...

22. B and D

Martin Gore and Alan Wilder are vegetarians. Gore since 1983, according to him, influenced by Gareth Jones during the mixing of *Construction Time Again* in Berlin.

23. B

Tona de Brett (1931-2021), author of the bestseller *Discover Your Voice. Learn to Sing from Rock to Classic* (Schott Music Ltd, 1996), whose lessons he would not have liked entirely. He was trying to improve his vocal performance in concert, in particular by controlling his breathing better so that he could run on stage between verses without his voice getting lost.

24. B

Chess.

25. D

16 January 1993 to be exact. They have two children, Megan and Joe.

26. D

Bananas.

27. B

Because of his propensity to come back to life after a near-death experience, as if he had the nine lives traditionally granted to cats (it is said that emergency doctors in Los Angeles nicknamed him this).

28. D

Callcott, the surname of Len, his biological father, before his mother Sylvia remarried (in 1964) to Jack Gahan, who adopted Dave and his sister.

29. C

This represents a traditional Celtic motif of stylised wings protecting against evil. Created in Los Angeles by father and son tattooists Bob and Charlie Roberts, according to Dave Gahan.

30. B

At Maida Vale.

31. C

A. Wilder's car (registration number J616CUC) was almost hit by a fighter plane, an RAF Tornado, which crashed into a hill in Glen Ogle, less than three hundred metres from his car, creating a crater nearly twenty metres wide at the side of the road and generating a shower of debris, some of which fell into his car. The pilot and co-pilot were unfortunately killed in the explosion. Alan Wilder refers to this tragedy in the track 'Black Box' on the album *Liquid* (2000) by Recoil, his personal music project.

32. C

A daughter, Paris (born in 1995) and a son, Stanley (born in 2001) with his second wife Hepzibah Sessa (who was a member of the Miranda Sex Garden group on the Mute label), with whom he remained married until 2010; and a daughter, Clara Lake (born in 2012) from his union with Norwegian Britt Rinde Hvål. The couple would buy a new house in Norway in 2024.

33. D

Jonathan Kessler has been their manager for decades. He joined their professional entourage in 1986 as an accountant (we can see him in the film *101* shuffling thousands of dollars). In 1994, he became their first (and only to date) manager. On 14 November 2017, he received the Peter Grant Award at the Artist and Manager Awards (AMA) in London.

34. D

Le Gascogne was located at 12 Bleinheim Terrace in London, not far from the famous Abbey Road in St John's Wood. A. Fletcher sold the restaurant around 2002.

35. A

This is the name D. Gahan gave to the house in Nichols Canyon where he lived in 1995, in the hills above Hollywood, because he had seen a large number of his "guests" turn a blue-purple colour as a result of their addiction to drugs and being on the verge of death. This is also the house that "friends" more or less emptied when he was in rehab, as they had become so accustomed to having access to rich junkie Gahan's house...

36. C

1 June 1995, the day Alan turned thirty-six. Daniel Miller and the members of the band had been warned beforehand. Although he played such a decisive role in developing the richness of DM's sound, in fact he was only in the band for thirteen years. Most fans, however, continue to show him unwavering devotion.

37. C

The Sunset Marquis Hotel.

38. D

Toast Hawaii. The name comes from a rather strange sandwich (sandwich bread, ham and pineapple) that he used to like in the cafeteria of the Hansa Tonstudios when the band was mixing *Construction Time Again* in Berlin. During these sessions, to relax, Andy Fletcher is said to have started recording an album of covers, provisionally called the 'Toast Hawaii Album', accompanied by Martin Gore on guitar and Alan Wilder on piano. But is there any physical evidence of this? A cassette was circulated and Daniel Miller wasn't very convinced by the result... On this label, Fletcher released two albums by the electro duo Client: *Client* (2003) and *City* (2004), a live album and a handful of EPs, and nothing else to date...

39. C

On a number of occasions he has used the pseudonym Client F, especially when supporting or working with his Toast Hawaii label band Client, whose two members used to be called Client A (Kate Holmes) and Client B (Sarah Blackwood).

40. D

Martin has two younger half-sisters (Karen and Jacqueline). Vince has an older sister (Carol) and two younger brothers (Michael and Rodney). Andy is the eldest of four (two sisters, Karen and Susan, and younger brother Simon). Dave has an older sister (Sue) and two younger half-brothers (Phil and Dan). Alan is the youngest of three brothers (Stephen and Andrew).

41. D

Faced with this disillusionment, which he almost felt to be a betrayal, he moved to the village of Erfde in the state of Schleswig-Holstein (in the north of Germany, two hours from Hamburg) where the farm of the Frenzen family is located, with whom he has kept in touch.

42. C

Dave Gahan, at least not publicly.

43. B

Martin Gore was married to Suzanne Boisvert from 1994 to 2004. And on 12 June 2014, on one of the Turks and Caicos Islands (in the British West Indies), he married Kerrilee Kaski, an American actress and producer born on 9 February 1981. Their relationship began in 2011.

44. B

Joanne – or Jo – Fox (1985-1991), Teresa Conroy (1992-1996) and Jennifer Sklias (since 1999).

45. C

Montauk.

46. C

Viva Lee, Ava Lee, Calo Leon, Johnnie Lee, Mazzy Lee. Three children with Suzanne Boisvert: daughters Viva Lee (1991), Ava Lee (1995) and son Calo Leon (2002). Then two daughters with his second wife Kerrilee Kaski: Johnnie Lee (2016) and Mazzy Lee (2017).

47. B

In 1999.

48. C

His personal recording studio, in his Santa Barbara villa.

49. C

7 November 2020. The 35th edition of the event took place live on HBO, and not in May as usual, because of the coronavirus pandemic. Depeche Mode was inducted by actress Charlize Theron. But the most notable feature was undoubtedly the conversation between the three members of the band, hilarious, each at home because of the confinements. In the video where Dave Gahan reads the acceptance speech, Martin Gore says he is rather relieved not to have to travel to Cleveland for the usual ceremony.

50. B

Andy Fletcher died on Thursday 26 May 2022.

Part II

DM ON RECORDS

01 *Which track did not appear on the **first tape of demos** that the band gave out to several London record labels in the second half of 1980?*

A) 'Factory' ☐
B) 'Just Can't Get Enough' ☐
C) 'Photographic' ☐
D) 'Dreaming of Me' ☐

02 *What was DM's **first song to be released** on record, in this case on the compilation* Some Bizzare Album, *released on Stevo's label on 30 January 1981?*

A) 'Dreaming of Me' ☐
B) 'Ice Machine' ☐
C) 'Photographic' ☐

03 *Stevo's* Some Bizzare Album *compilation features a number of **unknown bands** who were soon to make a name for themselves. Which one wasn't on this album?*

A) Blancmange ☐
B) Soft Cell ☐
C) Nick Cave and the Bad Seeds ☐
D) The The ☐

04 *What is Depeche Mode's **first single**?*

A) 'New Life' ☐
B) 'Just Can't Get Enough' ☐
C) 'Photographic' ☐
D) 'Dreaming of Me' ☐

05 *In November 1978, Daniel Miller created the **Mute Records label** to release his own first single 'T.V.O.D.' under the moniker The Normal. This is the number MUTE 001 in his catalogue. What was the number of DM's first single, 'Dreaming of Me', released by Mute in February 1981?*

A) Mute 009 ☐
B) Mute 011 ☐
C) Mute 013 ☐
D) Mute 015 ☐

06 *How many tracks on the **first album*** Speak & Spell *were written and/or composed by Martin Gore?*

A) 0 ☐
B) 1 ☐
C) 2 ☐
D) 4 ☐

07 *In 1981, 'Dreaming of Me', the band's first single, appeared on the German, French and American versions of their debut album* Speak & Spell, *although it did not appear on the original UK pressing.* ***Which song*** *did 'Dreaming of Me' take the place of on these continental and American versions of the album?*

A) 'Big Muff' ☐
B) 'Nodisco' ☐
C) 'I Sometimes Wish I Was Dead' ☐
D) 'What's Your Name?' ☐

08 *What is the title of the* ***B-side*** *to the single 'Leave in Silence'?*

A) 'Now, This is Fun' ☐
B) 'Oberkorn (It's a Small Town)' ☐
C) 'Excerpt from My Secret Garden' ☐
D) 'Any Second Now' ☐

09 *Where does the title '****Oberkorn****' come from, the track that appears on the B-side of the single 'The Meaning of Love' and whose title was, according to M. Gore, suggested to the record company on the spur of the moment?*

A) it's a reference to a brand of cereal ☐
B) it's a reference to a krautrock band ☐
C) it's a traditional German song ☐
D) it's a village in Luxembourg ☐

10 *The first recording with Alan Wilder is also the last one recorded at the* ***Blackwing Studios*** *in London. Which single is it?*

A) 'The Meaning of Love' ☐
B) 'Leave in Silence' ☐
C) 'Get the Balance Right' ☐
D) 'Love, in Itself' ☐

11 Construction Time Again *was largely recorded at* ***The Garden studio*** *in Shoreditch, East London, with Gareth Jones as sound engineer for the first time. Which musician owned this studio?*

A) John Foxx (Ultravox's first singer) ☐
B) the members of Genesis ☐
C) Peter Gabriel ☐
D) Dave Stewart (from Eurythmics) ☐

12 *The lyrics to many of the songs on* Construction Time Again, *such as 'Everything Counts', were written after* ***a tour of Asia*** *in April-May 1983. In which city did several members of the band experience a kind of awakening to the power of money and the exploitation of the masses?*

A) Seoul ☐
B) Bangkok ☐
C) Tokyo ☐
D) Hong Kong ☐

13 *Which of these songs was not* ***written and composed by Alan Wilder****?*

A) 'Pipeline' (1983) ☐
B) 'The Landscape is Changing' (1983) ☐
C) 'Two Minute Warning' (1983) ☐
D) 'In Your Memory' (1984) ☐

14 *The two songs written by Alan Wilder for* Construction Time Again *have something in common lyrically. What* ***essential concern*** *do these two texts suggest about their author?*

A) political concerns ☐
B) sexual concerns ☐
C) economic concerns ☐
D) ecological concerns ☐

15 *In the post-Clarke era,* Construction Time Again *is the only album from which only two singles have been released. Alan Wilder later hinted that one track in particular had been discussed as a potential* ***third single****, before the idea was dropped. Which album track was it?*

A) 'More Than A Party' ☐
B) 'And Then...' ☐
C) 'The Landscape is Changing' ☐
D) 'Told You So' ☐

16 *Between spring and the end of 1983, DM's last three singles were released in limited edition mini albums, with identical designs in* ***three colours****. Give each track its own colour:*

A) *Get the Balance Right and Live Tracks*	a) blue
B) *Everything Counts and Live Tracks*	b) green
C) *Love, in Itself, 2 and Live Tracks*	c) burgundy

17 *The* ***melodica*** *is a kind of harmonica with a keyboard. On which track does Martin Gore play it?*

A) 'Leave in Silence' ☐
B) 'Everything Counts' ☐
C) 'See You' ☐
D) 'People Are People' ☐

18 *Only three titles were* ***co-written by Martin Gore and Alan Wilder****, in 1983 and 1986. Which were they?*

A) 'The Great Outdoors!' ☐
B) 'Fools' ☐
C) 'Christmas Island' ☐
D) 'Work Hard' ☐

19 *On which of these five albums is there no* ***instrumental track****?*

A) *Speak & Spell* ☐
B) *A Broken Frame* ☐
C) *Some Great Reward* ☐
D) *Music for the Masses* ☐
E) *Ultra* ☐

20 *What is, unanimously, the band's* ***least favourite song*** *from their repertoire?*

A) 'Just Can't Get Enough' ☐
B) 'People Are People' ☐
C) 'See You' ☐
D) 'What's Your Name?' ☐

21 *What is the only track on the* Some Great Reward *album to be* ***penned by Alan Wilder****?*

A) 'Lie to Me' ☐
B) 'If You Want' ☐
C) 'Something to Do' ☐
D) 'People Are People' ☐

22 *Two **compilations** were released in North America in the mid-1980s so that new fans of the band could hear some tracks from the first albums which, when they were released in Europe, were not distributed on the American continent. What are these two compilations called?*

- A) *Catching Up with Depeche Mode* ☐
- B) *Old News from Depeche Mode* ☐
- C) *Masters of Mode* ☐
- D) *People Are People* ☐

23 *What is Depeche Mode's **tenth single**?*

- A) 'Love, in Itself' ☐
- B) 'People Are People' ☐
- C) 'Blasphemous Rumours' ☐
- D) 'Shake the Disease' ☐

24 *And what's the band's **twentieth single**?*

- D) 'A Question of Lust' ☐
- B) 'Never Let Me Down Again' ☐
- C) 'Behind the Wheel' ☐
- D) 'Personal Jesus' ☐

25 *According to Martin Gore, the* **Black Celebration** *album is the one that gave him the confidence to record more songs sung entirely by himself. How many does he sing on this album?*

A) 3 ☐
B) 4 ☐
C) 5 ☐
D) 6 ☐

26 *The title track from* Black Celebration *begins with a sort of* ***ironic summary*** *of the whole album, which is hard to hear and announces: "A brief period of rejoicing". If you listen very carefully, you'll recognise the voice of:*

A) Alan Wilder ☐
B) Martin Gore ☐
C) Andy Fletcher ☐
D) Daniel Miller ☐

27 *On 'Stripped', the start-up of a big car is sampled and can be heard very clearly at the beginning of the track. Which car was used for the sample?*

A) Alan Wilder's Mercedes ☐
B) a racing car hired by Daniel Miller ☐
C) Dave Gahan's Porsche ☐
D) Gareth Jones' Volvo ☐

28 *On the album* Black Celebration *(1986), a song scratches at the off-beat behaviour of the* ***British royal family****, referring with bitter irony to a dress affair. Which song is it?*

A) 'Blue Dress' ☐
B) 'New Dress' ☐
C) 'Dressed in Black' ☐

29 *Before 2006, what was the only single from the band to officially contain two A-sides, that is a* ***double A-sided single****?*

A) 'Love, in Itself' ☐
B) 'Master and Servant' ☐
C) 'Blasphemous Rumours' ☐
D) 'Never Let Me Down Again' ☐

30 *Which DM single finally had its* ***A and B sides reversed*** *for the American market (with a new cover), mainly under the influence of university radio stations, which played the B-side more than the A-side of the single imported from England?*

A) 'See You' / 'Now, This is Fun' ☐
B) 'It's Called a Heart' / 'Fly on the Windscreen' ☐
C) 'Stripped' / 'But Not Tonight' ☐
D) 'Behind the Wheel' / 'Route 66' ☐

31 *In 1986, Mute decided to release a* ***collector's version*** *of one of the singles from* Black Celebration, *which had been struggling to find a place in the hits parades. Until then, a new EP with a limited version had been enough to boost sales, but in this case, Mute went one step further: they released a 5-track cassette in a luxury box, containing a booklet with the lyrics and previously unpublished photos in a card sleeve that also contained a colour badge. Which single is it?*

A) 'Stripped' ☐
B) 'A Question of Lust' ☐
C) 'A Question of Time' ☐
D) 'But Not Tonight' ☐

32 *How many copies of* **Music for the Masses** *were sold in the USA?*

A) 500 000 ☐
B) plus d'1 million ☐
C) 2 millions ☐
D) plus de 2 millions ☐

33 *What does the title of the instrumental '**Agent Orange**', which first appeared on a 'Strangelove' EP, refer to?*

A) a famous Dutch secret agent often mentioned by Anton Corbijn ☐
B) a chemical used during the Vietnam War ☐
C) a brand of orange loudspeakers used on the band's visuals at the time ☐
D) a drug in orange capsules that circulated in techno clubs ☐

34 *How many singles were taken from the band's seventh studio album,* **Violator** *(1990), which contained only nine tracks?*

A) 2 ☐
B) 3 ☐
C) 4 ☐
D) 5 ☐

35 *According to Martin Gore, the title '**Personal Jesus**' refers to the surprising way in which a North American personality was called in the intimacy of his marriage. Who is it about?*

A) Elvis Presley ☐
B) Ronald Reagan ☐
C) Neil Young ☐
D) J. F. Kennedy ☐

36 *It's not uncommon for DM to need to go through* ***several studios*** *before producing a complete album. They are no exception in this respect. Which studio did the band not work in for the* Violator *album?*

A) Logic Studios (Milan) ☐
B) Puk Studios (Aarhus in Denmark) ☐
C) Axis (New York) ☐
D) Guillaume Tell (Suresnes near Paris) ☐

37 *Before writing which album did Martin Gore suffer a serious bout of* ***writer's block****?*

A) *A Broken Frame* (1982) ☐
B) *Music for the Masses* (1987) ☐
C) *Exciter* (2001) ☐
D) *Delta Machine* (2013) ☐

38 Violator *is one of the few albums, and especially the first, to have a* ***one-word title****. Why did the band choose this strange word to title the album?*

A) as a pun on the violet colour, A. Fletcher's favourite colour ☐
B) to pay tribute to an old American blues album much loved by M. Gore ☐
C) to parody the "destructive" titles of certain metal bands ☐
D) to shock the self-righteous virtue leagues ☐

39 *Which* ***producer*** *approached by Mute to produce what was to become the* Violator *album flatly refused the job?*

A) Steve Lillywhite ☐
B) Brian Eno ☐
C) Trevor Horn ☐
D) Dave Bascombe ☐

40 *Who uttered the phrase "If you wanna use* ***guitars****, use guitars" when recording* Violator*?*

A) Daniel Miller ☐
B) Andy Fletcher ☐
C) Flood ☐
D) Jonathan Kessler ☐

41 *In which song did DM use an* ***electric guitar*** *for the first time?*

A) 'Get the Balance Right' ☐
B) 'People Are People' ☐
C) 'Never Let Me Down Again' ☐
D) 'Personal Jesus' ☐

42 *Which of these songs is not an **instrumental**?*

A) 'Pimpf' ☐
B) 'Khaleid' ☐
C) 'Stjarna' ☐
D) 'Agent Orange' ☐
E) 'Poorman' ☐

43 *On which single, on the B-side of the 45-rpm EP, is Alan Wilder's piano interpretation of a **Beethoven sonata**, the 'Moonlight Sonata'?*

A) 'A Question of Lust' (1986) ☐
B) 'Strangelove' (1987) ☐
C) 'Little 15' (1988) ☐
D) 'Policy of Truth' (1990) ☐

44 *Which single kicked off the collaboration between **producer Flood** and Depeche Mode?*

A) 'It's Called a Heart' ☐
B) 'Stripped' ☐
C) 'Personal Jesus' ☐
D) 'Never Let Me Down Again' ☐

45 *In **which cities** were the following albums mainly recorded?*

A) *Songs of Faith and Devotion*	a) Santa Barbara
B) *Some Great Reward*	b) Madrid
C) *Exciter*	c) Aarhus (Denmark)
D) *Violator*	d) Berlin

46 *Martin Gore has confessed to having recorded one of the songs he sang in 1984 **completely naked**, in a small room in the basement of Hansa Studios in Berlin, which would have frightened a studio assistant a little, sent down there by the other members of the band with full knowledge of the facts. Which song is it?*

A) 'Somebody' ☐
B) 'Pipeline' ☐
C) 'It Doesn't Matter' ☐
D) 'Blasphemous Rumours' ☐

47 *Which of the band's singles features two previously **unreleased tracks on the B-side** of the single?*

A) 'See You' (1982) ☐
B) 'Little 15' (1988) ☐
C) 'World in My Eyes' (1990) ☐
D) 'It's No Good' (1997) ☐

48 *Which of the band's first six albums is the only one to contain a song with the* ***same title as the album****?*

A) *Speak & Spell* ☐
B) *A Broken Frame* ☐
C) *Construction Time Again* ☐
D) *Some Great Reward* ☐
E) *Black Celebration* ☐
F) *Music for the Masses* ☐

49 *DM have never been known for writing a plethora of songs for each new album. As a result, several of their albums contain just nine tracks. Which of the following albums (on LP vinyl) contains* ***more than nine tracks****?*

A) *A Broken Frame* ☐
B) *Construction Time Again* ☐
C) *Some Great Reward* ☐
D) *Violator* ☐

50 *In fact, only one of the four albums mentioned above actually contains* ***only nine tracks****, as the other two also feature a short instrumental cover of one of the flagship tracks. So, which one really only contains nine tracks?*

A) *Some Great Reward* ☐
B) *Construction Time Again* ☐
C) *Violator* ☐

51 *After which album did **Daniel Miller** clearly disengage himself from studio recording work, offering the band professional producers?*

A) *Some Great Reward* ☐
B) *Black Celebration* ☐
C) *Music for the Masses* ☐
D) *Violator* ☐

52 *It's common knowledge that the recording of* **Songs of Faith and Devotion** *in a villa in the Madrid region was not without its ups and downs. Dave Gahan, in particular, was not well at all and regularly skipped the recording sessions. What did he spend a lot of time doing?*

A) leaving the villa and riding his quad bike through the olive groves ☐
B) playing video games alone in his room ☐
C) shutting himself up in his room to paint ☐
D) spending his time by (and in) the pool ☐

53 *On which track from* Songs of Faith and Devotion *were the three* ***gospel soloists*** *Hildia Campbell, Bazil Meade and Samantha Smith invited to accompany the group?*

A) 'Rush' ☐
B) 'One Caress' ☐
C) 'Get Right With Me' ☐
D) 'In Your Room' ☐

54 *Which instrument was **Steáfán Hannigan** invited to play on 'Judas' from* Songs of Faith and Devotion*?*

A) drums ☐
B) English horn ☐
C) uilleann pipe ☐
D) viola da gamba ☐

55 *When most albums were only released on CD, it became fashionable to include tracks on the albums that were not listed in the track list, known as "hidden tracks". DM has not resisted the temptation to include unlisted instrumentals on some albums. What is the title of the **hidden track** on* Ultra*?*

A) 'Painkiller' ☐
B) 'Junior Painkiller' ☐
C) 'Slowblow' ☐

56 *Which of the five historic members who took part in studio recordings has **never signed a single DM track**?*

A) Vince Clarke ☐
B) Andy Fletcher ☐
C) Dave Gahan ☐
D) Martin Gore ☐
E) Alan Wilder ☐

57 *Which DM studio album contains the highest number of tracks with a* ***single word*** *in the title?*

A) *Sounds of the Universe* ☐
B) *Exciter* ☐
C) *Music for the Masses* ☐
D) *Delta Machine* ☐
E) *Speak & Spell* ☐

58 *How many Depeche Mode records in 25 cm format (or 10 inches) have been officially released by Mute?*

A) 0 ☐
B) 1 ☐
C) 2 ☐
D) 3 ☐

59 *Quite a few singers and groups have used and abused the song with a* ***female first name*** *as its title, such as Leonard Cohen's famous 'Suzanne'. If DM has done it, how many times has it been used?*

A) 0 ☐
B) 1 ☐
C) 2 ☐
D) 3 ☐

60 *What is the title of the Dave Gahan song that could be called* ***the song of discord*** *because it was categorically refused by Martin Gore when D. Gahan proposed it during the* Ultra *sessions in 1997, which led to a nagging grudge on his part?*

A) 'The Home Song' ☐
B) 'The Sad Song' ☐
C) 'The Ocean Song' ☐
D) 'The Sky Song' ☐

61 *How many* ***hidden tracks*** *does the CD version of* Exciter *(2001) contain?*

A) 0 ☐
B) 1 ☐
C) 2 ☐
D) 3 ☐

62 *It's the Depeche Mode single that's by far the* ***biggest seller*** *in Mute's entire catalogue. Which one do you think it is?*

A) 'Everything Counts' ☐
B) 'People Are People' ☐
C) 'Personal Jesus' ☐
D) 'Enjoy the Silence' ☐

63 *Which of these Depeche Mode singles was the first to have lyrics written by singer* ***Dave Gahan****?*

A) 'Shake the Disease' (1985) ☐
B) 'Never Let Me Down Again' (1987) ☐
C) 'Barrel of a Gun' (1997) ☐
D) 'Suffer Well' (2006) ☐

64 *Before 2023, only one song was* ***co-written by Martin Gore and Dave Gahan****. Which song is it?*

A) 'Hole to Feed' ☐
B) 'Fragile Tension' ☐
C) 'Peace' ☐
D) 'Oh Well' ☐

65 *What are the only three of the band's singles* ***sung by Martin Gore*** *to date?*

A) 'Somebody', 'A Question of Time', 'It Doesn't Matter Two' ☐
B) 'Somebody', 'A Question of Lust', 'Love, in Itself' ☐
C) 'Somebody', 'Sacred', 'Home' ☐
D) 'Somebody', 'A Question of Lust', 'Home' ☐

66 *In between albums, or before the release of a compilation, Mute pushes the band to release singles. How many* **non-album singles** *have they produced?*

A) 2 ☐
B) 4 ☐
C) 6 ☐
D) 8 ☐

67 *Which single did the band release on 30 October 2006 to accompany the compilation* **The Best of Depeche Mode, Volume 1**, *released a fortnight later?*

A) 'Suffer Well' ☐
B) 'Martyr' ☐
C) 'Precious' ☐

68 *Which DM album features songs* **written by Dave Gahan** *for the first time?*

A) *Ultra* ☐
B) *Exciter* ☐
C) *Playing the Angel* ☐
D) *Sounds of the Universe* ☐

69 *Give each album back its **main producer**:*

A) *Songs of Faith and Devotion* — a) Mark Bell
B) *Sounds of the Universe* — b) James Ford
C) *Exciter* — c) Flood
D) *Spirit* — d) Ben Hillier

70 *If we take for granted Martin Gore's words, only one album was recorded **without any real tension** within the band. Which one was it?*

A) *Exciter* ☐
B) *Playing the Angel* ☐
C) *Sounds of the Universe* ☐
D) *Spirit* ☐

71 *What's the **longest period of time** between the release of two DM studio albums?*

A) 4 years ☐
B) 5 years ☐
C) 6 years ☐
D) 7 years ☐

72 *What was the **first track** on these four albums?*

A) *Exciter*
B) *Delta Machine*
C) *Some Great Reward*
D) *Sounds of the Universe*

a) 'Something to Do'
b) 'In Chains'
c) 'Dream On'
d) 'Welcome to My World'

73 *Which of these tracks **closes a DM studio album**?*

A) 'World Full of Nothing' ☐
B) 'Nothing to Fear' ☐
C) 'Clean' ☐
D) 'Nothing' ☐

74 *On the* **Delta Machine** *album (2013), which track follows the title 'Should Be Higher'?*

A) 'My Little Universe' ☐
B) 'Alone' ☐
C) 'Goodbye' ☐
D) 'Soothe My Soul' ☐

75 *The B-side of the single '**A Pain That I'm Used to**' (2005) is:*

A) 'Ghost' ☐
B) 'Newborn' (Foster Remix) ☐
C) 'Never Let Me Down Again' (Digitalism Remix) ☐
D) 'The Darkest Star' (Monolake Remix) ☐

76 *At the beginning of 2024, just about ten months after its release, the* **Memento Mori** *album already contained four singles. Only one of them was never released on physical media (and was therefore only a digital file). Which was it?*

A) 'Wagging Tongue' ☐
B) 'Ghosts Again' ☐
C) 'My Favourite Stranger' ☐
D) 'Speak to Me' (HI-LO Extended Remix) ☐

77 *According to their record company, how many records did the band **sell worldwide**?*

A) 50 million ☐
B) 75 million ☐
C) 100 million ☐
D) 200 million ☐

78 *How many* ***studio albums*** *has the band released to date?*

A) 14 ☐
B) 15 ☐
C) 16 ☐
D) 17 ☐

79 *And how many* ***singles****?*

A) 41 ☐
B) 51 ☐
C) 61 ☐
D) 71 ☐

80 *How many* ***tracks*** *(with different titles) has the band officially released to date (i.e. October 2024)?*

A) 174 ☐
B) 236 ☐
C) 274 ☐
D) 324 ☐

1. B

'Just Can't Get Enough'. This appears to have been the tape that V. Clarke and D. Gahan, who were in charge of canvassing record labels directly, offered to an overworked Daniel Miller at Rough Trade, who didn't take the time to listen to it.

2. C

This was the first version of 'Photographic', the second track on Side A, among other bands who, like them, had not yet released an album. Released on the Some Bizzare Records label founded by Stephen John Pearce, known simply as Stevo.

3. C

Nick Cave and the Bad Seeds are not included. DM's 'Photographic' is number two on Side A, called *Fish Side*, just after Illustration's 'Tidal Flow', a band that soon faded into obscurity. The The's 'Untitled' came third. Blancmange's 'Sad Day' and Soft Cell's 'The Girl with the Patent Leather Face' appear on the B-side (called the *Eye Lamp Side*). This was Stevo's first release on his brand new Some Bizzare Records label.

4. D

'Dreaming of Me'.

5. C

Mute 013.

6. C

Two: 'Tora! Tora! Tora!' and the instrumental 'Big Muff'; the others are by Vince Clarke.

7. C

'I Sometimes Wish I Was Dead'.

8. C

'Excerpt from My Secret Garden'.

9. D

Oberkorn is the name of a small town in Luxembourg where the band played a memorable concert, due to the incongruous nature of the venue, on 30 March 1982 in a club called the Rainbow Club, during the continental leg of the "See You Tour".

10. C

'Get the Balance Right', recorded in December 1982 and released on 31 January 1983, was the first use of the expensive and complicated Synclavier II that Daniel Miller had just invested in, much to Alan Wilder's delight.

11. A

The Garden was also the title of John Foxx's 1981 album, following the success of his 1980 *Metamatic*. Genesis' studio was called The Farm, in Surrey. Peter Gabriel didn't open his own, Real World Studio (in

Wiltshire, not far from Bath), until 1986. DM only used Dave Stewart's Church Studio (in Crouch End, north London) at the end of 1989, to finish mixing the *Violator* album with Flood.

12. B

In Bangkok, Thailand. They played two concerts there, on 9 and 10 April 1983 at Napalai Hall.

13. A

'Pipeline'.

14. D

Alan Wilder's cry for ecology awareness is very clear in both 'Two Minute Warning' and 'The Landscape is Changing'.

15. B

'And Then...' Surprisingly, a promotional 7" of 'Told You So' (identical A and B sides: 'Told You So'/'Te Lo Dije Asi') was released by RCA in Spain at the end of 1983, to promote four concerts in Spain in February 1984. The dates and cities appear on the red-and-white sleeve of this rare record.

16. A-a / B-c / C-b.

17. B

It was a melodica by Hohner that popularised the concept.

18.

A: 'The Great Outdoors' / **C**: 'Christmas Island' / **D**: 'Work Hard'. **B** is by Alan Wilder alone. A fourth track was co-written by the two members of DM with a third man, Daniel Miller: 'Black Day' on the B-side of the 1986 EP 'Stripped'.

19. C

Some Great Reward (1984).

20. D

'What's Your Name?' on *Speak & Spell* (1981). The lyrics of the chorus of Vince Clarke ("Hey you're such a pretty boy") are said to be a tongue-in-cheek reference to the fact that journalist Rick Sky of the *Daily Star* tabloid had turned his words into an article, pretty much saying that bands with ugly members couldn't be successful. This mortified Vince Clarke to the point where he didn't leave his flat for days, according to Deb Danahay, his girlfriend at the time.

21. B

'If You Want'.

22. A and D

Catching Up with Depeche Mode was released in North America on 11 November 1985 by Sire Records. As for *People Are People*, it was a compilation released in the United States and Canada by Sire Records on 2 July 1984, mainly to relaunch the group's career after the commercial failure of the 1983 album *Construction Time Again*, even though the spring 1984 single 'People Are People' had shown promise in the United States.

23. B

'People Are People' is their tenth single, released on 12 March 1984.

24. C

'Behind the Wheel' is the band's twentieth single, released on 28 December 1987.

25. B

Four songs. 'A Question of Lust', 'Sometime', 'It Doesn't Matter Two', 'World Full of Nothing'. You could add the bonus track 'Black Day' from the CD version.

26. D

Daniel Miller uses a passage from Prime Minister Winston Churchill's famous speech announcing the end of the Second World War in Europe on Tuesday 8 May 1945: "We may allow ourselves a brief period of rejoicing, but let us not forget for a moment the toils and efforts that lie ahead".

27. C

It was Dave Gahan's Porsche that was recorded and sampled (I have no proof that Gareth Jones owned a Volvo at the time the *Black*

Celebration album was recorded...).

28. B

'New Dress' is about Lady Di buying a new dress when the world around her is showing worrying signs of dysfunction. **C** is also on *Black Celebration* and **A** is on the *Violator* album.

29. C

This is the single 'Blasphemous Rumours' / 'Somebody', reference Mute 7 BONG 7, the band's twelfth single released on 29 October 1984: A: 'Somebody' (Remix); AA: 'Blasphemous Rumours' (black sleeve). This single also exists in a four-song version (yellow sleeve, 7 BONG 7 E) with the above-mentioned tracks on side A and two live tracks on side B: 'Told You So' and 'Everything Counts'. This is the only example of a DM 7" disc with 4 tracks.

30. C

'Stripped' / 'But Not Tonight'. The cover is the same, but white rather than black. [See also question 8, part V].

31. B

'A Question of Lust', reference C BONG 11, released in April 1986. Side A: 'A Question of Lust' remix by Flood and 'Christmas Island'. Side B: 'If You Want', 'Shame' and 'Blasphemous Rumours', three tracks recorded live on 30 November 1984 in Basel, Switzerland. The tape was also released on vinyl, but only in Germany (reference INT

126.844 – Mute C BONG 11).

32. B

Over a million. The record came with *Violator*, which sold three million copies in the United States.

33. B

It was a defoliant that was one of six "rainbow herbicides" produced by the chemical companies Dow Chemical and Monsanto (although the chemical was created in the 1950s) for the US army, which used them during the Vietnam War (from 1961 to 1971) to destroy vegetation, with the aim of limiting the Viet Cong's camouflage and depleting its agricultural resources. This highly toxic product was actually between pink and brown in colour, but owed its name to the orange paint stripes on the storage drums. The track appears on the limited-edition EP L12 BONG 13, released in May 1987 by Mute. Surprisingly, on the French version of the limited-edition EP (Virgin reference 80315), 'Agent Orange' lasts just 4 minutes (1'03 less than the version on the English EP, but also less than the version on the German EP – ref. INT 126.866). The track was then included as a bonus track on the CD version of *Music for the Masses*.

34. C

Four singles from *Violator*: 'Personal Jesus', 'Enjoy the Silence', 'Policy of Truth', 'World in My Eyes'.

35. A

In her book *Elvis & Me* (1985), Priscilla Presley recounts how she used the affectionate nickname "Personal Jesus" to refer to her husband Elvis in private.

36. D

Guillaume Tell (the former art deco cinema Le Capitole in Suresnes near Paris).

37. C

For *Exciter*, and it was Daniel Miller's advice that got him off the hook: to go straight into the studio without any real songs, with two collaborators capable of coming up with exciting ideas, in this case Paul Freegard and Gareth Jones.

38. C

To parody the "destructive" titles of certain metal bands. The band have made it clear on several occasions that most of their album titles are ironic and often misunderstood. The only other one-word album titles are *Ultra* (1993), *Exciter* (2001) – in the same spirit of mischievous derision as *Violator* – and *Spirit* (2017).

39. B

Brian Eno. Dave Bascombe was not available to return to the studio after his work that the band had enjoyed on *Music for the Masses*. So Flood (Mark Ellis) was chosen. Nevertheless, in 1993 Brian Eno took part in two remixes of the single 'I Feel You': 'I Feel You (Life's Too Short Mix)' and 'I Feel You (Swamp Mix)' on the L12 BONG 21 EP released on 15 February 1993.

40. C

It was Flood who encouraged them in this way and relieved Martin Gore, who wanted to push his use of electro blues-style guitars further in 'Personal Jesus'. The phrase became famous as the title of the short film on the DVD accompanying the deluxe version of the 2006 reissue of *Violator.*

41. A

It's 'Get the Balance Right' with a guitar sound played by Martin Gore and transformed electronically, as Andy Fletcher testifies in Jonathan Miller's *Stripped: Depeche Mode.*

42. E

'Poorman' is sung by D. Gahan on the album *Spirit* (2017).

43. C

'Little 15' (1988).

44. B

In 1986, Mark Ellis, aka Flood, was commissioned to produce an extended version of the single 'Stripped'. The result was the version known as 'Stripped (Highland Mix)', released on 8 March 1986 (reference 12 BONG 10). The previous year he had only been given a B-side: he had remixed 'Flexible (Remixed Extended Version)' for the 'Shake the Disease' EP (12 BONG 8) released on 29 April 1985.

45. A-b / B-d / C-a / D-c.

46. A

'Somebody'. This is Stefi Marcus, tape operator, who must still remember it. There were no witnesses because this room in the basement was not connected by video to the control room where the others were. Martin Gore recounts the anecdote in a long interview with the band for *Melody Maker* (22 September 1984).

47. C

This is 'World in My Eyes', with two tracks recorded during the *Violator* album sessions on the B-side: 'Happiest Girl' and 'Sea of Sin'. Fourth and final single from *Violator*, released on 17 September 1990.

48. E

Black Celebration in 1986, which never happened again. Album titles are generally expressions that appear in the text of one of the songs.

49. A

The album *A Broken Frame* (1982) contains ten tracks.

50. A

Some Great Reward. On *Construction Time Again*, at the end of side B, there's a 59-second reprise of the main theme from 'Everything Counts'. On *Violator*, there are even two instrumental interludes: just after 'Enjoy the Silence', over a minute and forty seconds of instrumental known as 'Interlude #2 (Crucified)', and following 'Blue Dress' another instrumental track (about 1'20) known as 'Interlude #3'.

51. B

Black Celebration (1986).

52. C

He often shut himself up in his room to indulge a fairly recent passion, painting.

53. C

On 'Get Right With Me'. Campbell and Smith were also present on the tour on this track and on 'Condemnation'.

54. C

The uilleann pipe is a type of Irish bagpipe.

55. B

'Junior Painkiller', which lasts 2'10, is linked to 'Insight' at the end of the B-side. Then on the digital and CD versions, the song appears with its title as the final track. 'Painkiller' and 'Slowblow' are two longer instrumentals, recorded during the same sessions, and appear as bonus tracks on the 2007 deluxe CD reissue.

56. B

Andy Fletcher did not sign any DM tracks.

57. D

Delta Machine contains 7 one-word tracks, if you count 'Always' which doesn't appear on all versions of the album. *Sounds of the Universe* contains 6; *Exciter*, 5; *Music for the Masses*, 4, as do *Playing the Angel* and *Spirit*. *Speak & Spell* contains 3, as does *Songs of Faith and Devotion*. The other albums contain just one or two, and *Memento Mori* is the only one without a song having a single word title.

58. B

Only one: this is the EP released in February 1989 with, on the A-side, 'Everything Counts' in the "Absolut Mix" version by Alan Moulder, followed by 'Everything Counts' in the "1983 12" Mix" version, and on the B-side 'Nothing' in the "US 7" Mix" version by Justin Strauss, followed by 'Everything Counts (Reprise)'. Numbered on the bottom right of the black sleeve and catalogued 10 BONG 16, sold with two postcards and a sticker.

59. C

Only 'Lilian" (*Playing the Angel*) and 'Jezebel' (*Sounds of the Universe*) fall into this category, although the latter is more of a biblical reference than a purely feminine one. 'Caroline's Monkey' on *Memento Mori* does not, of course, fall into the category of a first name used alone.

60. C

'The Ocean Song' has become 'Closer' and appears as an unreleased track with 'Breathe' on the mini CD of 'I Need You' (CD reference Mute 301) from 2003.

61. A

Zero.

62. D

Especially since 'Enjoy the Silence' was released in a number of formats in February 1990 (ref. BONG 18) and was re-released in October 2004 as 'Enjoy the Silence.04' (ref. BONG 34). Corbijn's iconic video clip, which was blasted on every music channel in the world, led by MTV, undoubtedly played a big part in the song's success.

63. D

'Suffer Well' (2006). Since the departure of Vince Clarke in 1981, all the singles had been written by Martin Gore. Only a few B-sides had been collaborative ('Work Hard' on the B-side of 'Everything Counts' was co-written by Gore and Wilder) or signed by Alan Wilder: 'Fools' on the back of 'Love, in Itself', 'In Your Memory' on the back of 'People Are People'.

64. D

'Oh Well' is the B-side of the single 'Wrong' (2009), which would have greatly deserved more exposure. **A** is by Gahan alone. **B** and **C** are by

Gore. A second track co-written by the duo has since appeared on *Memento Mori*: 'Wagging Tongue'.

65. D

'Somebody', 'A Question of Lust', 'Home'. The first: 'Somebody' (which was coupled on a double A-side single with 'Blasphemous Rumours' sung by Dave Gahan, the band's twelfth single, released on 29 October 1984). The second: 'A Question of Lust' (the band's sixteenth single, released on 14 April 1986). And the third: 'Home' (the band's thirty-third single, released on 16 June 1997).

66. C

Six: 'Dreaming of Me' (1981), 'Get the Balance Right' (1983), 'Shake the Disease' and 'It's Called a Heart' (1985), 'Only When I Lose Myself' (1998) and 'Martyr' (2006).

67. B

This is the 45th single, 'Martyr', which doesn't appear on any studio album.

68. C

Playing the Angel (2005) with three compositions by Dave Gahan in association with Christian Eigner and Andrew Phillpott: 'Suffer Well', 'I Want It All' and 'Nothing's Impossible'. In order to play a full part in the album, Dave Gahan, who had just proved himself with his first solo album, demanded that half the tracks be his own, which Gore could not accept. Producer Ben Hillier came up with a compromise of three tracks.

69. A-c / B-d / C-a / D-b.

70. C

It was *Sounds of the Universe*, so much so that M. Gore also said that, for the first time, the band felt a certain sadness when the record was completed. *Spirit* was undoubtedly one of the worst recordings along with *Songs of Faith and Devotion*, with producer James Ford acting as mediator on several occasions, even threatening to call the whole thing off because of the intense communication problems between the band members.

71. C

It's a six-year gap between the albums *Spirit* (2017) and *Memento Mori* (2023). Between the four albums on the band's debut, there was a gap of one year only! Two years, for the first time, between *Some Great Reward* (1984) and *Black Celebration* (1986). Then it was three years between *Music for the Masses* (1987) and *Violator* (1990) and *Songs of Faith and Devotion* (1993). Then a certain norm established itself around four years, between *Songs of Faith and Devotion* (1993) and *Ultra* (1997), between *Exciter* (2001) and *Playing the Angel* (2005) then *Sounds of the Universe* (2009), or between *Delta Machine* (2013) and *Spirit* (2017).

72. A-c / B-d / C-a / D-b.

73. C

'Clean' is the last track on *Violator* (1990).

74. B

'Alone'.

75. B

'Newborn' (Foster Remix).

76. D

'Speak to Me', a version called "HI-LO Extended Remix", available digitally from August 2023.

77. C

100 million.

78. B

15 studio albums.

79. C

61 singles.

80. B

236 tracks.

Part III

DM VISUAL

01 *When did the band get two parts of the* ***holy grail*** *that almost every British band just starting out dreams of?*

A) first appearance on *Top of the Pops* (BBC)
B) first *NME* cover

a) 22 January 1981
b) 25 June 1981
c) 22 August 1981
d) 25 January 1982

02 *What is the only official video for a single featuring* ***Vince Clarke****?*

A) 'Dreaming of Me' ☐
B) 'New Life' ☐
C) 'Just Can't Get Enough' ☐

03 *During a TV appearance on a programme to promote the single 'See You', Dave, Martin, Andy and then Alan successively hold* ***a farm animal*** *in their hands while singing (in playback). Which animal is it?*

A) a rabbit ☐
B) a hen ☐
C) a duck ☐
D) a piglet ☐

04 *What album cover doesn't use a* ***photo by Brian Griffin****, a Birmingham photographer who shot a lot of record albums in the 1980s and 90s?*

A) *Speak & Spell* ☐
B) *Construction Time Again* ☐
C) *Black Celebration* ☐
D) *Violator* ☐

05 *What's the video in which Dave Gahan buys the very 45-rpm of the title track, in a rather phony* ***mise en abyme*** *filmed by Julien Temple?*

A) 'Just Can't Get Enough' ☐
B) 'See You' ☐
C) 'The Meaning of Love' ☐
D) 'Get the Balance Right' ☐

06 *In which official video, directed by Clive Richardson, are the members of the group operating a whole range of machines on a* ***warship****?*

A) 'Love, in Itself' ☐
B) 'Everything Counts' ☐
C) 'Master and Servant' ☐
D) 'People Are People' ☐

07 *At the start of their career, which song did they have to playback in the castle gardens of the famous* ***Alton Towers theme park*** *as part of the TV show* Hold Tight*?*

A) 'See You' ☐
B) 'Leave in Silence' ☐
C) 'Everything Counts' ☐
D) 'Love, in Itself' ☐

08 *On the cover of* Some Great Reward*, bottom right, a newly-wed couple strike the pose against a backdrop of a bluish industrial site. The young man undoubtedly looks like* ***Alan Wilder****. Is it Alan?*

A) yes ☐
B) no ☐

09 *What is the title of the first Depeche Mode* ***VHS video cassette*** *released by Mute in 1985?*

A) *Some Great Videos* ☐
B) *Strange* ☐
C) *Strange Too* ☐
D) *The World We Live In And Live In Hamburg* ☐

10 *What was the name of the artist who* ***designed the cover art*** *for the singles 'Shake the Disease' and 'It's Called a Heart' in 1985?*

A) Tina Kitaro ☐
B) Tamara Capellaro ☐
C) Hilda Catriano ☐
D) Alba Hidalgo ☐

11 *Only one of the band's singles features a real* ***animal on its cover****. Which one?*

A) 'The Meaning of Love' ☐
B) 'It's Called a Heart' ☐
C) 'Just Can't Get Enough' ☐
D) 'Walking in My Shoes' ☐

12 *In which video do the band members appear on a quay in* ***London's docks****, filmed as if they were falling horizontally in slow motion?*

A) 'Stripped' ☐
B) 'People Are People' ☐
C) 'Shake the Disease' ☐
D) 'It's Called a Heart' ☐

13

Who designed the cover for **Music for the Masses***?*

A) Brian Griffin ☐
B) Martyn Atkins ☐
C) Anton Corbijn ☐
D) Peter Saville ☐

14

What was the first studio album cover to feature ***the band in the photo*** *on the back?*

A) *Speak & Spell* ☐
B) *Construction Time Again* ☐
C) *Music for the Masses* ☐
D) *Ultra* ☐

15

And what's the only studio album to feature the band members ***on the front cover****?*

A) *A Broken Frame* ☐
B) *Black Celebration* ☐
C) *Songs of Faith and Devotion* ☐
D) *Delta Machine* ☐

16 *Even though he sometimes photographed the band as part of his work for the* New Musical Express *(NME) back in 1981, when did* ***Anton Corbijn*** *become particularly associated with Depeche Mode's image, by directing the music video?*

A) 'It's Called a Heart' (1985) ☐
B) 'A Question of Time' (1986) ☐
C) 'Strangelove' (1987) ☐
D) 'Enjoy the Silence' (1989) ☐

17 ***Which group*** *had Anton Corbijn worked with extensively before approaching DM and shaping their image for a long time to come?*

A) Simple Minds ☐
B) New Order ☐
C) U2 ☐
D) The Cure ☐

18 *Not many fans know the name* ***Jane Spiers****. However, before the Corbijn era, she played a crucial role in DM's concert set design, designing the lighting effects and projections, notably on the "Some Great Reward Tour". What nationality was this young woman?*

A) American ☐
B) Australian ☐
C) New Zealander ☐
D) South African ☐

19 *Which member of the band is posing* ***opposite a naked woman****, whose back is shown on the back cover of the legendary single 'Personal Jesus'?*

A) Andy Fletcher ☐
B) Dave Gahan ☐
C) Martin Gore ☐
D) Alan Wilder ☐

20 *How was everyone able to preview the '****Personal Jesus****' single in August 1989?*

A) by turning up at a specific church in central London ☐
B) by going to Mute Records dressed as Jesus ☐
C) by dialling a phone number written in a classified ad ☐

21 *In which video do the members of the group have their* ***faces completely painted*** *in a different colour?*

A) 'Leave in Silence' ☐
B) 'Get the Balance Right' ☐
C) 'Stripped' ☐
D) 'A Question of Lust' ☐

22 *Several albums have a slogan on the back cover that sums up the tone of the record, usually with a touch of irony. To which albums do the following four* **slogans** *belong?*

A) "Life in the so-called space age" — a) *Sounds of the Universe*
B) "The world we live in and life in general" — b) *Black Celebration*
C) "Spreading the news around the World" — c) *Music for the Masses*
D) "Songs in the key of space" — d) *Some Great Reward*

23 *Finally, on the back of which album do we read the slogan: "***Pain and suffering in various tempos***"?*

A) *Construction Time Again* ☐
B) *Exciter* ☐
C) *Playing the Angel* ☐
D) *Delta Machine* ☐

24 *Which is the only one of the four singles on the* Ultra *album not to have been directed by Anton Corbijn, but by* **Steve Green***?*

A) 'Barrel of a Gun' ☐
B) 'It's No Good' ☐
C) 'Home' ☐
D) 'Useless' ☐

25 *When the band appeared on* **Top of the Pops** *on 14 February 1997 to promote 'Barrel of a Gun', there were five of them on stage. Who was behind the drums?*

A) Daniel Miller ☐
B) Alan Wilder ☐
C) Christian Eigner ☐
D) Anton Corbijn ☐

26 *Who directed the video for '**Only When I Lose Myself**' in 1998?*

A) Clive Richardson ☐
B) Brian Griffin ☐
C) Anton Corbijn ☐
D) Peter Care ☐

27 *Who is the **French director** of the video for 'Dream On',* Exciter*'s first single?*

A) Olivier Assayas ☐
B) Stéphane Sednaoui ☐
C) Jean-Baptiste Mondino ☐
D) Michel Gondry ☐

28 *On which **single cover** did the band first appear?*

A) 'The Meaning of Love' (1982) ☐
B) 'It's Called a Heart' (1985) ☐
C) 'In Your Room' (1994) ☐
D) 'Barrel of a Gun' (1996) ☐

29 *For years, the group's songs have attracted **advertisers** to promote a whole range of products: cars, perfumes, clothes... Some are direct DM songs, others are covers. Find out which product needed each of these songs to sell better:*

A) 'Personal Jesus'	a) GAP clothing (1999)
B) 'People Are People'	b) perfume Parisienne by Yves Saint-Laurent (2009)
C) 'Just Can't Get Enough'	c) Peugeot SUV (2019)
D) 'Enjoy the Silence'	d) Renault Kangoo E-Tech (2023)
E) 'I Feel You'	e) Volkswagen Golf VII (2012)

30 *And in which **car advert** is Dave Gahan even behind the wheel?*

A) Volkswagen Golf VII (2012) ☐
B) Peugeot SUV (2019) ☐
C) Renault Kangoo E-Tech (2023) ☐

31 *In which video does Dave Gahan sing while dancing in a sometimes creepy way, with his eyes closed but with* ***pupils painted on his eyelids****?*

A) 'I Feel You' ☐
B) 'Barrel of a Gun' ☐
C) 'Condemnation' ☐

32 *In which video is Martin Gore disguised as* ***Andy Fletcher's bride-to-be*** *in a wedding dress shop window?*

A) 'The Meaning of Love' ☐
B) 'Strangelove' ☐
C) 'Suffer Well' ☐

33 *In which video are the* ***cheesy Depeche Mode*** *playing in a seedy cabaret, ushered on stage by a pitiful host in a grey suit over a shirt with a tartan collar, who drops his microphone and is none other than Anton Corbijn?*

A) 'It's No Good' ☐
B) 'Ghosts Again' ☐
C) 'Walking In My Shoes' ☐

34 *In which video does a moustachioed Dave Gahan stroll through the streets clad like an* ***astronaut****?*

A) 'Wagging Tongue' ☐
B) 'Precious' ☐
C) 'Cover Me' ☐

35 *On the back cover of* Playing the Angel, *Martin Gore is wearing a T-shirt featuring an* ***English band****. This band is:*

A) The Clash ☐
B) Birthday Party ☐
C) Sex Pistols ☐
D) The Cure ☐

36 *Which DM video has been nominated for a Grammy Award in the* **best short film** *category?*

A) 'Peace' by Jonas & François ☐
B) 'Fragile Tension' by Rob Chandler & Barney Steel ☐
C) 'Wrong' by Patrick Daughters ☐
D) 'Where's the Revolution' by Anton Corbijn ☐

37 ***Dozens of books*** *have been written about the group. Several are of great interest. Name the author of these four notable titles, published in recent years:*

A) *Depeche Mode Monument*
B) *Depeche Mode. The Biography*
C) *Stripped: Depeche Mode*
D) *Depeche Mode. Faith & Devotion*

a) Jonathan Miller
b) Ian Gittins
c) Steve Malins
d) Dennis Burmeister and Sascha Lange

38 *How much does the book Depeche Mode by Anton Corbijn, published by* ***Taschen*** *in 2021, weigh?*

A) 1.1 kg ☐
B) 2.2 kg ☐
C) 3.3 kg ☐
D) 4.4 kg ☐

39 *Which French* ***ready-to-wear brand*** *did Dave Gahan model for in 2017?*

A) Lacoste ☐
B) Dior Homme ☐
C) Louis Vuitton ☐
D) Yves Saint Laurent ☐

40 *Four video clips were shot for songs from the* **Memento Mori** *album in 2023 and 2024. Dave Gahan and Martin Gore only play in one of them. In which song?*

A) 'Ghosts Again' ☐
B) 'Wagging Tongue' ☐
C) 'Before We Drown' ☐
D) 'People Are Good' ☐

1.

A-b: 'New Life'. The single – their second – had been released two weeks earlier. It was such a success that they returned to play it twice at *Top of the Pops*, on 16 and 30 July 1981. It reached number 11 in the charts / **B-c**: On the cover of the 22 August 1981 issue of *NME*, with two lines of headlines at the bottom: "Depêche In The Flesh / In The Middle Of The Môde", and with a photo by Anton Corbijn already. Dave Gahan, in pink shirt, braces and bluish tie, appears blurred in the foreground, and the other three, clear and laughing, against a white wall in the background. Gahan would have held a grudge against Corbijn for a long time.

2. C

In the clip for 'Just Can't Get Enough' directed by Clive Richardson. No video for DM until this 3rd single.

3. B

Hens! Gahan and Fletcher are wearing suits and ties like young provincial bankers, while Gore and Wilder are wearing bow ties. Broadcast on 27 April 1982 on the German channel ARD's *Bananas* programme (a music programme broadcast from 1981 to 1984 featuring many international artists).

4. D

Violator (1990).

5. B

It's in 'See You' that D. Gahan, strolling through a department store, picks up a copy of 'See You' in the 45-rpm section before proceeding to the checkout with it. The *mise en abyme* is supported by the fact that, in the aisles, the band members and several extras spend their time pressing the keys of various keyboards, including Alan Wilder, who makes his first appearance in an official DM video. Perhaps surprisingly today, 'See You' was the band's highest charting single in the early years (6th place), and the first to be written by M. Gore. Released on 29 January 1982, it was followed by a short world tour, the "See You Tour". Julien Temple also directed the video for 'The Meaning of Love' a few months later.

6. D

In 1984, the group is filmed on board the warship HMS Belfast, a 1938 cruiser that is now a museum ship on the River Thames.

7. B

This was for 'Leave in Silence' in September 1982 and the show was broadcast on 4 October. Like all pop bands in their early days, DM had to comply with requests to appear on TV shows that they would have turned down if they'd had more bottle or if they hadn't used all the means at their disposal to make a name for themselves. *Hold Tight*, on Granada Television, was a programme for young people in the UK, where they made two appearances in 1982 and 1983 that the band members still laugh about. The setting for the filming was the famous Alton Towers theme park (in Staffordshire), actually situated in the grounds of an old castle, with its avenues, rockeries, orangeries, etc. The performance for 'Leave in Silence' (the first of their two appearances) is particularly memorable, as they were asked to walk around with their hands almost in their pockets, posing in several bucolic spots in the park while they were supposed to sing and play their song. Some lovely photos of this session can be found on the Internet... The following year (*Hold Tight*, 16 August 1983), they returned to Alton Towers Park for 'Everything Counts' in a slightly more conventional playback...

8. B

The couple are played by extras. Brian Griffin is very clear and precise on this subject. In several interviews on Vaughn George's YouTube channel, he details his work for the band. He is adamant that no member of the band was ever present at the photoshoot for any of the covers he did. The cover of *Some Great Reward* is particularly close to his heart, because the photos were taken at the Round Oak Steelworks near Dudley (in the Black Country, not far from Birmingham, where he was born), which had just closed and where he had worked for a time as a young man, and above all, at the steelworks he could see from his bedroom window as a child! The site has since become Merry

Hill Shopping Centre. Many fans also thought they recognised Alan Wilder's profile in the kissing couple on the cover of the 1986 single 'A Question of Lust' (and despite denials, some female fans even went into hysterics, as an article in the German magazine *Bravo* in the spring of 1986 testified).

9. D

The World We Live In And Live In Hamburg was released in April 1985, while *Some Great Videos* was released in October 1985. **B**: 1988 and **C**: 1990. It immortalised the concert at Hamburg's Alsterdorfer Sporthalle on 9 December 1984 during the "Some Great Reward Tour". The title uses words from the song 'Somebody'.

10. B

British painter, illustrator and sculptor Tamara Capellaro has illustrated a number of children's books and poetry. Her drawings of characters and animals in motion have made the covers in question iconic.

11. C

A cat appears on the cover of the single 'Just Can't Get Enough' (1981).

12. C

This is the video for 'Shake the Disease' directed by the Englishman Peter Care (born 1953), who had just made the successful video for Killing Joke's 'Love Like Blood'. He also filmed the clips for 'It's Called a Heart' and 'Stripped' the following year.

13. B

Martyn Atkins.

14. D

They first appeared on the back of *Ultra* in 1997.

15. C

On the front, they first appeared on *Songs of Faith and Devotion* in 1993, in stylized portraits by Corbijn. Apparently, the only photo of the band specially taken for a cover was for the compilation *The Singles 81-85*, by Eric Watson in 1985. Very early in their career, Dave Gahan made it clear that they didn't want to appear on albums because photos quickly make records go out of fashion, because of the frozen-in-time look. He cites Duran Duran's first album (June 1981) as an example not to be followed, because its photo has almost become a caricature of the New Romantics...

16. B

'A Question of Time', filmed in July 1986 by A. Corbijn near Los Angeles between two concerts on the US tour. The single was officially released on Monday 11 August 1986.

17. C

U2.

18. C

New Zealander. She was in charge of the lighting from the "Construction Time Again Tour" onwards, and then of the sets up until the *Violator* tour.

19. C

It's Martin Gore. D. Gahan appears on the back of the 45-rpm EP. A. Wilder on the back of the CD single. Finally, A. Fletcher appears, like the other three members, on the limited-edition 7" with gatefold sleeve (reference G BONG 17).

20. C

Mute's sales department had a small, cryptic message printed in the classified section of several British newspapers. It was four lines of white text in a square with a black background: Your Own / PERSONAL / JESUS / (01) 675 22 77. When the number was dialled, an answering machine played the song with the unstoppable refrain "Reach out and touch faith". Some newspapers immediately stopped publishing the advert when it became known that it was disguised promotion on the part of the music industry...

21. A

In 'Leave in Silence', a video directed by Julien Temple, Dave's face is painted blue, Andy's yellow, Martin's red and Alan's green. They wear white outfits and bounce coloured balloons. In another sequence in the clip, they use wooden spoons and percussion sticks to smash everyday objects as they move along a conveyor belt covered with a white tablecloth.

22. A-b / B-d / C-c / D-a.

23. C

Playing the Angel (2005).

24. C

'Home', released on 16 June 1997, featured a video by Steve Green, for a shorter version of the track than on the album.

25. D

Anton Corbijn really seems to be playing! For this first single without Alan Wilder, the configuration of the band on stage had to be greatly modified. Tim Simenon, producer of the *Ultra* album due for release a month later, also appears on keyboards.

26. B

This is Brian Griffin (1948-2024), who designed so many covers for the band before the Corbijn era. This is the only DM video he ever directed.

27. B

Stéphane Sednaoui was born in 1963 and has dual French-American nationality. Clips for U2, Björk, Garbage, Red Hot Chili Peppers...

28. D

'Barrel of a Gun' (1996).

29.

A-c / **B-e** (the various characters sing the song right to the end and it's the original song that you hear) / **C-a** / **D-d** (Moriarty's cover from 2007) / **E-b**.

30. A

Volkswagen Golf VII (2012).

31. B

In the video for 'Barrel of a Gun' directed by A. Corbijn in 1997.

32. C

In the video for 'Suffer Well' directed by A. Corbijn in 2006.

33. A

In the video for 'It's No Good' directed by A. Corbijn in 1997.

34. C

In the video for 'Cover Me' directed by A. Corbijn in 2017.

35. C

This is a T-shirt representing Queen Elizabeth II on the cover of 'God Save the Queen' single by the Sex Pistols (1977).

36. C

That was on 3 December 2009. This video was also ranked second in *Time* magazine's top five music videos of 2009.

37.

A-d (Blumenbar, 2013) / **B-c** (Andre Deutsch Ltd, 1999) / **C-a**(Omnibus Press, 2003) / **D-b** (Palazzo Editions, 2019).

38. C

A 512-page, 3.3 kg book in 24.3 x 34 cm format, sold for 100 euros. A cheaper paperback version was later published.

39. B

Designer Kris Van Assche has chosen to mark ten years working for the Dior Homme brand by asking Dave Gahan to model the autumn-winter 2017 collection, with photos taken by British photographer David Sims.

40. A

D. Gahan and M. Gore appear from start to finish in the video for 'Ghosts Again' directed by Anton Corbijn. But there's also a wink in 'Wagging Tongue' (video by The Sacred Egg and Corbijn) where they appear in a single blurred shot.

Part IV

DM LIVE

01 *Who were Depeche Mode supporting when* ***Daniel Miller*** *first saw them on stage on 12 November 1980, before deciding to offer them a contract to release a single?*

A) Wire ☐
B) Fad Gadget ☐
C) D.A.F. ☐
D) Cabaret Voltaire ☐

02 *Where did Depeche Mode play its* ***first concert outside the UK*** *before the release of its first album?*

A) Dublin, Ireland ☐
B) Berlin, Germany ☐
C) The Hague, Netherlands ☐
D) Brussels, Belgium ☐

03 *The fourteen-date UK tour for the* Speak & Spell *album ran from 31 October to 16 November 1981. Keeping his promise, Vince Clarke took part even though he had announced to the band and Daniel Miller that he was leaving DM more than a month earlier. How many of the* ***fourteen concerts*** *were sold out?*

A) zero ☐
B) six ☐
C) twelve ☐
D) fourteen ☐

04 *Friday 2 April 1982 at Le Palace was Depeche Mode's second Paris concert (the first had been at Les Bains Douches on 29 September 1981). Which* ***French band*** *opened for them?*

A) Taxi Girl ☐
B) Indochine ☐
C) Starshooter ☐
D) Bijou ☐

05 *What year was their first (short)* ***American tour****?*

A) 1981 ☐
B) 1982 ☐
C) 1983 ☐
D) 1984 ☐

06 *In which* ***London venue*** *were the twelve live tracks featured on the B-sides of the three mini-albums with blue, green and burgundy sleeves released in 1983?*

A) The Roundhouse ☐
B) Hammersmith Odeon ☐
C) The Royal Albert Hall ☐
D) Brixton Academy ☐

07 *When did they first **perform in Ireland**?*

A) around the time of *Speak & Spell* ☐
B) around the time of *A Broken Frame* ☐
C) around the time of *Construction Time Again* ☐

08 *When was DM's first **sold-out concert in Paris**?*

A) 17 December 1984 (Bercy) ☐
B) 6 May 1986 (Bercy) ☐
C) 16 November 1987 (Bercy) ☐

09 *When was DM's **first concert in Australia**?*

A) 31 August 1985 ☐
B) 31 August 1987 ☐
C) 31 August 1990 ☐

10 *Everyone remembers the **Live Aid concerts** held simultaneously at London's Wembley Stadium and Philadelphia's John F. Kennedy Stadium on Saturday 13 July 1985. Which concerts did Depeche Mode take part in?*

A) London ☐
B) Philadelphia ☐
C) neither ☐

11 *In what year did the band play its first concert on the other side of what was known as the **Iron Curtain**, before the fall of the Berlin Wall, to designate the countries of the Communist bloc?*

A) 1983 ☐
B) 1985 ☐
C) 1988 ☐
D) 1990 ☐

12 *On the "Music for the Masses Tour", Dave Gahan was dressed in a **single colour from head to toe** (except for his shoes!): trousers, shirt, short tank top. Which colour was it?*

A) black ☐
B) white ☐
C) red ☐
D) navy blue ☐

13 *Why is their first live album, recorded at the Rose Bowl in Pasadena (California) on 18 June 1988 (and released in 1989), called* **101***?*

A) to celebrate the legendary Route 101 ☐
B) because the "Music for the Masses Tour" included 101 dates ☐
C) as a tribute to the band Electribe 101 who sometimes supported them ☐
D) because their show lasted exactly 101 minutes ☐

14 *This concert was the subject of the film* 101 *by American director D. A. Pennebaker (1925-2019), also released in March 1989. Which* ***legendary North American artist*** *had he previously filmed on tour?*

A) Johnny Cash ☐
B) Bob Dylan ☐
C) Elvis Presley ☐
D) Neil Young ☐

15 *In this film, Alan Wilder explains and demonstrates some of the* ***synth*** *parts he plays on a particular track. Which song is it?*

A) 'Strangelove' ☐
B) 'Everything Counts' ☐
C) 'Black Celebration' ☐
D) 'Never Let Me Down Again' ☐

16 *Which singer did Dave Gahan spend a lot of time with backstage on the night of the concert at the* ***Rose Bowl in Pasadena****?*

A) Bono ☐
B) Johnny Cash ☐
C) Axl Rose ☐
D) Bruce Springsteen ☐

17 *Which of these bands has* ***never opened*** *for DM on one of their tours?*

A) Algiers ☐
B) D.A.F. ☐
C) Electribe 101 ☐
D) Simple Minds ☐
E) Nitzer Ebb ☐
F) Orchestral Manoeuvres in the Dark ☐

18 *Which* ***instrumental piece*** *was used as an introduction to the concert on the following tours?*

A) "Music for the Masses Tour"	a) 'Kaleid'
B) "A Broken Frame Tour"	b) 'Christmas Island'
C) "Black Celebration Tour"	c) 'Oberkorn (It's A Small Town)'
D) "World Violation Tour"	d) 'Pimpf'

19 *On the "**Devotional Tour**" for* Songs of Faith and Devotion, *which instrument did Alan Wilder play on stage in four and then six consecutive songs?*

A) guitar ☐
B) bass ☐
C) drums ☐
D) piano ☐

20 *At the end of the concert at London's Crystal Palace on 31 July 1993, before leaving the stage, the singer of the opening act made a derogatory comment to the 35,000-strong audience: "And now enjoy the **puppet show**!" Who was this disrespectful person?*

A) Matt Johnson from The The ☐
B) Mark E. Smith from The Fall ☐
C) Andrew Eldritch from The Sisters of Mercy ☐
D) Wayne Hussey from The Mission ☐

21 *What is special about the live album* **Songs of Faith and Devotion Live...** *released in 1993?*

A) the screams from the crowd were completely removed in the studio ☐
B) it contains only the 10 tracks from the *Songs of Faith and Devotion* album ☐
C) the tracks on it were all recorded at different concerts ☐

22 *Which support band did DM ask to leave the* Songs of Faith and Devotion *tour, because they couldn't stand being* ***booed by the crowd*** *eager to see the headliner?*

A) Spiritualized ☐
B) Primal Scream ☐
C) Miranda Sex Garden ☐
D) An Emotional Fish ☐

23 *During which* Songs of Faith and Devotion *concert did Dave Gahan* ***fracture his ribs*** *when he missed his stage diving at the end of the song 'A Question of Time' during the final encore?*

A) 25 June 1993 in Stuttgart ☐
B) 15 September 1993 in Toronto ☐
C) 28 June 1994 in Philadelphia ☐
D) 8 July 1994 in Indianapolis ☐

24 *Which tour saw Andy Fletcher* ***return to England*** *for treatment for depression and be replaced on keyboards, more or less at short notice, by Daryl Bamonte?*

A) "Music for the Masses Tour" (1987-1988) ☐
B) "World Violation Tour" (1990) ☐
C) "Devotional Tour" (1993) ☐
D) "Exotic Tour/Summer Tour '94" (1994) ☐
E) "The Singles Tour" (1998) ☐

25

Has the band ever played ***concerts in Africa****?*

A) yes ☐
B) no ☐

26

What was the only DM studio album that ***didn't tour****?*

A) *Construction Time Again* ☐
B) *Violator* ☐
C) *Ultra* ☐
D) *Playing the Angel* ☐

27

As for Dave Gahan, he only toured for one of his two solo albums, Paper Monsters *(2003) and* Hourglass *(2007). Which of the two was supported by more than* ***seventy concert dates****?*

A) *Paper Monsters* ☐
B) *Hourglass* ☐

28 *Dave Gahan and Martin Gore's solo albums were released less than three months apart in 2003. With each of them supporting their albums with a tour, Martin and Dave naturally performed a few DM songs live on stage. Here are* ***six DM songs*** *heard at these concerts. Who sang them?*

A) 'Only When I Lose Myself' / 'In Your Room' / 'Shake the Disease'
B) 'Policy of Truth' / 'Never Let Me Down Again' / 'Enjoy the Silence'

a) Martin Gore
b) Dave Gahan

29 *When did Alan Wilder join his three former bandmates on stage at a* ***charity concert*** *in London to play 'Somebody' on the piano with Martin Gore singing?*

A) 17 February 2005 ☐
B) 17 February 2010 ☐
C) 17 February 2015 ☐
D) 17 February 2020 ☐

30 *During which tour did the band play a* ***concert in Abu Dhabi*** *in the United Arab Emirates for the only time in their career?*

A) "Exotic Tour/Summer Tour '94" (1994) ☐
B) "The Delta Machine Tour" (2013-2014) ☐
C) "Global Spirit Tour" (2017-2018) ☐
D) "Memento Mori World Tour" (2023-2024) ☐

31

*Which of these **guitars** did Martin Gore never play live?*

A) Gretsch G5810 Bo Diddley Signature rectangular ☐
B) Gibson Red Firebird III Non-Reverse ☐
C) First Act Star Guitar ☐
D) Fender Stratocaster 1973 Black Maple ☐

32

Which of these four songs does Martin Gore regularly play live with his iconic green Gretsch guitar (the Gretsch G6118 Double Anniversary)?

A) 'I Feel You' ☐
B) 'Stripped' ☐
C) 'Enjoy the Silence' ☐
D) 'Home' ☐

33

*How many times has DM played at the **Stade de France** in Saint-Denis near Paris?*

A) 2 ☐
B) 3 ☐
C) 4 ☐
D) 5 ☐

34 *Which tour was not followed by a **live DVD**?*

A) "Touring the Angel" (2005-2006) ☐
B) "Tour of the Universe" (2009-2010) ☐
C) "The Delta Machine Tour" (2013-2014) ☐
D) "Global Spirit Tour" (2017-2018) ☐
E) "Memento Mori World Tour" (2023-2024) ☐

35 *In which city was the concert recorded that serves as the basis for **Anton Corbijn's film*** Spirits in the Forest – A Depeche Mode Film *which was shown in cinemas around the world on 21 November 2019?*

A) Berlin ☐
B) Barcelone ☐
C) Paris ☐
D) Mexico ☐

36 *For* Spirits in the Forest, ***six fans from around the world*** *were selected to be filmed by Anton Corbijn and his team, from their homes to the venue of the final concert of the "Global Spirit Tour". Who's the odd one out?*

A) Carine, the Frenchwoman ☐
B) Christian, the Romanian ☐
C) Daniel, the Brazilian ☐
D) Dicken, the Colombian ☐
E) Indra, the Mongolian ☐
F) Karl, the German ☐
G) Liz, the American ☐

37 *In which city did the "**Memento Mori World Tour**" start on 23 March 2023?*

A) Cologne ☐
B) Sacramento ☐
C) Paris ☐
D) Montreal ☐

38 *According to The Setlist Wiki (setlist.fm), here are the **four countries** where Depeche Mode have played most often, in alphabetical order. Now give them in order of importance:*

A) Germany	a) 98 times
B) United States	b) 233 times
C) France	c) 216 times
D) United Kingdom	d) 433 times

39 *What was Andy Fletcher's **favourite song** on which the band is paying tribute to Andy 'Fletch' Fletcher throughout the "Memento Mori World Tour" in 2023-2024?*

A) 'Walking in My Shoes' ☐
B) 'I Feel You' ☐
C) 'World in My Eyes' ☐
D) 'Everything Counts' ☐

40 *What musician's accessories did Martin Gore **donate to charity** after the "Memento Mori World Tour"?*

A) three signed guitar straps ☐
B) used guitar strings ☐
C) the sleeveless waistcoat he wore on stage ☐
D) two pairs of ankle boots worn on tour ☐

1. B

Fad Gadget. It was at The Bridgehouse pub in Canning Town (an East London district). To complete the circle, Fad Gadget supported DM on part of the *Exciter* tour of Europe in September and October 2001. Frank Tovey, aka Fad Gadget, died of a heart attack the following year at the age of 45.

2. C

On 25 July 1981, the band played at the Parkpop Festival at the Zuiderpark in The Hague, as part of their "New Life Tour". (This was the first Parkpop Festival – now held at the end of June – and they played before Tuxedomoon). DM returned to play in the Netherlands on 26 September 1981, at the Paradiso in Amsterdam, and the concert was recorded by a local radio station. Remember that their debut album *Speak & Spell* was not released until 5 October 1981.

3. C

Twelve of the fourteen concerts were sold out. The first took place at Newcastle University and the last two at the Lyceum in London. The duo Blancmange played as support act and travelled in the same minibus as DM. Vince Clarke's departure was not publicly announced until 30 November.

4. B

Indochine.

5. B

1982. In January, a handful of dates, including two (on the 22nd and 23rd) at The Ritz in New York. Then, in May 1982, came the "See You Tour" with eight dates in the U.S., with stops in Chicago, Los Angeles and New York, in clubs (like The Ritz in New York) rather than large concert halls, to promote the single 'See You' and the album *A Broken Frame*. All this before a bigger American tour in March 1985, after the "Construction Time Again Tour" had been cancelled at the end of 1983 following poor sales of the album across the Atlantic.

6. B

At Hammersmith Odeon, in the same concert on 25 October 1982, during the "Broken Frame Tour". [See also question 16 in Part II.]

7. B

At the time of *A Broken Frame*. DM played on 6 October 1983 in Dublin (National Stadium), the following day in Cork (City Hall) and on 8 October in Galway (Leisure Land), the last leg of the tour leaving Dave Gahan with a very bad memory as he was spat on from the first songs by a few rough guys in the front row.

8.

A : During the "Some Great Reward Tour". The concert was originally scheduled for 18 December 1984 at the Espace Balard (posters attest to this), but tickets unexpectedly sold out, so the Zénith was considered, and it was finally Bercy that hosted this first major episode in the French consecration. **B**: Two dates at Bercy for the "Black Celebration Tour" (6 and 7 May 1986). **C**: Two dates at Bercy for the "Music for the Masses Tour" (16 and 17 November 1987).

9. C

In fact, Depeche Mode only toured Australia twice: the first time was a one-off gig in Sydney (Hordern Pavilion) on 31 August 1990, during the "World Violation Tour" (followed by six dates in Japan!). Their second visit to Australia was in 1994, when they played five dates between 5 and 2 March: in Perth, Adelaide, Melbourne, Brisbane and Sydney (as part of their "Exotic Tour/Summer Tour '94").

10. C

They were not invited to take part in Live Aid, the aim of which was to raise funds to combat the famine in Ethiopia. Alan Wilder explained that if the band had been, there was a good chance they would have turned it down. That day, the band played in France, at the Breton festival Rockscène (previously known as Élixir) in Guéhenno, Morbihan (twelve tracks in a set lasting around fifty-five minutes). Also on the bill were The Clash, Leonard Cohen, The Ramones, Midnight Oil, Spear of Destiny and a few others.

11. B

At the end of the "Some Great Reward Tour", DM played two concerts in Eastern Europe: on 23 July 1985 in Budapest, Hungary (Volan Stadium), and on 30 July in Warsaw, Poland (Torwar Hall). They crossed the Iron Curtain again in 1988: a historic concert in East Berlin on 7 March, followed by two concerts in Budapest on 9 and 10 March, then a concert in Prage (Czechoslovakia at the time) on 11 March. The concert in East Berlin was organised by the state-run Free German Youth movement for 6,500 privileged people who were finally able to share what fans in West Germany had already experienced. The Berlin Wall came down in November 1989.

12. B

A white outfit.

13. B

Because the "Music for the Masses Tour" had 101 dates. The title was suggested by Alan Wilder.

14. B

Bob Dylan. It's from the film *Don't Look Back* (1967), which recounts Bob Dylan's UK tour in 1965. Donn Alan Pennebaker has also filmed Otis Redding, David Bowie and Alice Cooper. For *101*, he worked with two other directors, his wife Chris Hegedus and David Dawkins.

15. C

Black Celebration.

16. A

Bono, lead singer of U2.

17. D

Simple Minds.

18. A-d / B-c / C-b / D-a.

19. C

The drums. On (with a few variations at certain concerts) 'I Feel You', 'Never Let Me Down Again', 'Rush', 'In Your Room' and 'Personal Jesus', as featured in the *Devotional* video (1993), then 'Stripped' and 'Halo' as the tour progressed.

20. C

It was the last concert of the European leg of the "Devotional Tour", which doesn't resume until 6 September in Quebec. The Sisters of Mercy were the opening act on this night only...

21. B

It contains only the ten tracks from the album of the same title and in the same order, recorded live (produced and mixed by Alan Wilder and Steve Lyon largely in Dublin, at Windmill Lane Studios). Martin Gore was clearly not keen on the idea of releasing the live album in this way, but was persuaded to do so by the other members of the band.

22. A

Spiritualized had to throw in the towel after six concerts. The other groups mentioned also opened at one point or another on this colossal tour of 157 dates over thirteen months, between May 1993 and July 1994.

23. D

It was 8 July 1994, during the last concert of the "Exotic Tour/Summer Tour '94" in Indianapolis (Deer Creek Music Centre). At the end of 'A Question of Time', the sixteenth and final song, while jumping into the crowd Dave Gahan, more or less, fell between the stage and the security barrier. He was so high on drugs that he didn't really feel any pain and had no idea he'd bled internally... Since they were celebrating the end of the tour, a lot of strange things happened that night. When Alan Wilder started on 'Somebody' in the encore, he was surprised to see one of the team's technicians emerge from the piano where he himself had just been sitting. Incidentally, this was Alan Wilder's very last concert with Depeche Mode.

24. D

After two months, Andy Fletcher, suffering from psychological problems, left the tour. He was replaced by Daryl Bamonte, a technician who had been close to the band for years, for the following dates, from April to 8 July 1994, coached in a few days by Alan Wilder.

D. Bamonte played his first concert in São Paulo on 4 April.

25. A

Yes, only in South Africa. They played ten concerts on the "Exotic Tour/Summer Tour '94" between 9 and 26 February 1994: seven dates in Johannesburg, two in Cape Town and one in Durban.

26. C

Ultra. After Gahan's debauchery, overdoses and suicide attempts, Gore's alcoholism and drug addiction, Fletcher's depression (and Wilder's departure), nobody in the band or in their entourage thought that surviving another tour would be possible.

27. A

Paper Monsters.

28. A-a / B-b.

"A Night with Martin L. Gore" was Gore's only solo tour, with eight dates between 22 April (Stockholm) and 7 May 2003 (Los Angeles), accompanied by Peter Gordino and Andrew Phillpott, in support of his cover's album *Counterfeit*[2]. D. Gahan's "Paper Monsters Tour" included seventy-five concerts between 5 June (Zurich) and 30 November 2003 (Barcelona). The only DM track in common was 'Walking in My Shoes', which the two solo touring artists each sang a few times.

29. B

17 February 2010. The event was the Teenage Cancer Trust charity concert at London's Royal Albert Hall. It was during the encore that Alan Wilder took to the stage, for the 19th of the 22 songs the band played that night. On his website, he went on to say that he had been contacted a few weeks earlier by Dave Gahan on behalf of the whole band.

30. B

As part of "The Delta Machine Tour", DM played on 3 November 2013 at the "du Arena" on the island of Yas totally dedicated to tourism, sport and leisure.

31. D

Martin Gore has never been seen on stage on tour with a Strat': this is one of those particularly favoured by U2's The Edge. Martin Gore has used his grey rectangular Gretsch (**A**) on tour, on 'A Pain That I'm Used To' (2005) and on 'Come Back' and 'Corrupt' (2009-2010). He pulled out his red Gibson (**B**) on 'In Chains' (2009-2010 tour) and 'A Question of Time' (2013-2014 tour), for example. As for his First Act Star Guitar (**C**), he used it on the last tour for 'It's No Good' and 'John the Revelator'.

32. B

On 'Stripped' Martin Gore is on keyboards, so he's not using his

Gretsch G6118 Double Anniversary Green Knight.

33. C

Four times: "Tour of the Universe", June 2009; "Delta Machine Tour", June 2013; "Global Spirit Tour", July 2017; "Memento Mori Tour", June 2023.

34. E

No live show DVD for the 2023-2024 tour; it would be too expensive, A. Corbijn is quoted as saying... As a reminder, **A**: *Touring the Angel, Live in Milan* (2006, directed by Blue Leach); **B**: *Tour of the Universe: Barcelona 20/21.11.09* (2010, directed by Russel Thomas); **C**: *Live in Berlin: A Film by Anton Corbijn* (2014); **D**: *LiVE SPiRiTS* (2020, directed by Anton Corbijn and accompanying his 2019 film *Spirits in the Forest*).

35. A

During the "Global Spirit Tour", this documentary film shows the final concert at Berlin's Waldbühne, while following the stories of six fans of different nationalities. It was available on DVD the following June (2020).

36. F

No German Karl in the film...

37. B

The tour kicked off in Sacramento, followed by nine other dates in the United States and Canada before moving on to Europe. The 112th and final concert took place in Cologne on 8 April 2024.

38.

United States, 433 concerts (**B-d**); United Kingdom, 233 concerts (**D-b**); Germany, 216 concerts (**A-c**); France, 98 concerts (**C-a**).

39. C

'World in My Eyes'.

40. B

At the end of the "Memento Mori World Tour", Martin Gore donated his guitar strings to The Guitarwrist. The Guitarwrist is a British non-profit organisation that makes original and unique jewellery from the metal strings. The jewellery is then sold to raise funds for the charity Music Support, which helps people in the music industry, particularly those suffering from mental illness. Two professional jewellers are involved in the project: Emma Hedley Jewellery and Breakbeat Jewellery.

Part V

DM & CO.

01 *Of these four English singers, find the only one that Dave Gahan hasn't claimed as a* ***strong influence****:*

A) David Bowie ☐
B) Gary Numan ☐
C) Robert Smith from The Cure ☐
D) Dave Vanian from The Damned ☐

02 *When he left DM in November 1981,* ***Vince Clarke*** *immediately formed a duo with a female singer who had also grown up in Basildon. Which one did he choose?*

A) Alison Moyet ☐
B) Annabella Lwin ☐
C) Annie Lennox ☐
D) Anne Clark ☐

03 *Early in their career, the band covered '****The Price of Love****' quite often, including – and probably for the last time – during the encores of the short* Speak & Spell *tour in November 1981. Which American artists composed this song in 1965?*

A) The Beach Boys ☐
B) Simon & Garfunkel ☐
C) Creedence Clearwater Revival ☐
D) The Everly Brothers ☐

04 *To earn a living in the music business, Alan Wilder worked at DJM Studios on New Oxford Street in London. This led him to become an occasional* ***studio musician****. He took part in the recording of several albums and singles between 1979 and 1981. Which band didn't he record with?*

A) The Korgis ☐
B) Blancmange ☐
C) The Hitmen ☐
D) Real to Real ☐

05 *From the time of the* Construction Time Again *album, Martin Gore spent more and more time in Berlin, but it was in London in March 1983 that he was stunned to attend the first concert of a* ***German group*** *who were to influence him for several tracks on this album, released in August 1983. Who was this band?*

A) D.A.F. ☐
B) Nina Hagen ☐
C) Einstürzende Neubauten ☐
D) Die Toten Hosen ☐

06 *Started in 1986, long before he left DM, Alan Wilder led a* ***solo project*** *until 2012. What name did he choose?*

A) Coil ☐
B) Recoil ☐
C) This Mortal Coil ☐
D) Decoil ☐

07 *After DM, Vince Clarke went on to form several duos, many of which scored hit after hit. Which singer did he form these* ***three duets*** *with?*

A) The Assembly	a) Andy Bell
B) Erasure	b) Alison Moyet
C) Yazoo	c) Feargal Sharkey

08 *'But Not Tonight', the B-side of the single 'Stripped', was used on the soundtrack of an American* ***romantic comedy*** *released in December 1986. What was it called?*

A) *Pretty in Pink* ☐
B) *Modern Girls* ☐
C) *The Breakfast Club* ☐

09 *Under the name Recoil, Alan Wilder released two mini-albums in 1986 and 1987, entitled* 1+2 *(two tracks) and* Hydrology *(three tracks), which were followed by four more substantial albums, still on Mute, containing more tracks featuring guest singers. Could you put these four* ***Recoil albums*** *in chronological order?*

A) *Unsound Methods* ☐
B) *Liquid* ☐
C) *SubHuman* ☐
D) *Bloodline* ☐

10 *In June 1989, Martin Gore released* **Counterfeit e.p.** *on Mute, an unexpected mini album of cover versions of songs he had loved, many of them little-known. There are six of them, including the traditional song 'Motherless Child', which closes the B-side. Who are the other five songs by?*

A) 'Compulsion'	a) The Duruttti Column
B) 'In A Manner of Speaking'	b) Sparks
C) 'Smile in the Crowd'	c) The Comsat Angels
D) 'Gone'	d) Joe Crow (from The Nightingales)
E) 'Never Turn Your Back on Mother Earth'	e) Tuxedomoon

11 *Which* ***producer*** *is working with Martin Gore in the studio on his* Counterfeit e.p. *mini-album project?*

A) Flood ☐
B) Rico Conning ☐
C) François Kevorkian ☐
D) Daniel Miller ☐

12 *In 1991, **Wim Wenders** asked Depeche Mode to contribute to the soundtrack of his feature film. Martin Gore composed the track 'Death's Door', which he sang himself. Which film is it?*

A) *Until the End of the World* ☐
B) *Wings of Desire* ☐
C) *The End of Violence* ☐
D) *Faraway, So Close!* ☐

13 *In the **Leonard Cohen** tribute album* Tower of Song: The Songs of Leonard Cohen, *released by A&M Records in September 1995, which track is performed by Martin Gore?*

A) 'Suzanne' ☐
B) 'Bird on a Wire' ☐
C) 'Coming Back to You' ☐
D) 'I'm Your Man' ☐

14 *Which band asked **Alan Wilder** to join them on keyboards shortly after he announced his departure from Depeche Mode?*

A) Simple Minds ☐
B) Erasure ☐
C) The Cure ☐
D) New Order ☐

15 *Which of the following six artists has not officially recorded and released a* ***DM track****?*

A) The Cure ☐
B) Johnny Cash ☐
C) Marilyn Manson ☐
D) Rammstein ☐
E) Simple Minds ☐
F) Clan of Xymox ☐

16 *What song does Dave Gahan perform on the compilation of* ***Roxy Music*** *covers* Dream Home Heartaches... Remaking/Remodeling Roxy Music *(1997) put together by Duran Duran bassist John Taylor?*

A) 'Love Is The Drug' ☐
B) 'Ladytron' ☐
C) 'Virginia Plain' ☐
D) 'A Song for Europe' ☐

17 *Which DM song was covered by what critics sometimes considered – somewhat foolishly, it has to be said – to be their **enemy brothers** in the 80s, namely The Cure, on the 1998 CD* For the Masses (Tribute to Depeche Mode)*?*

A) 'Personal Jesus' ☐
B) 'Shake the Disease' ☐
C) 'World in My Eyes' ☐
D) 'Never Let Me Down Again' ☐

18 *On Martin Gore's second covers album,* Counterfeit², *released in 2003, how many tracks are **not sung in English** (and are therefore instrumentals or sung in other languages)?*

A) 0 ☐
B) 1 ☐
C) 2 ☐
D) 3 ☐

19 *How many albums (not counting singles) has Martin Gore released **outside DM** to date?*

A) 1 ☐
B) 2 ☐
C) 4 ☐
D) 5 ☐

20

*What nationality is **Christian Eigner**, DM's drummer on stage and occasionally in the studio since 1997?*

A) Austrian ☐
B) German ☐
C) Dutch ☐
D) American ☐

21

*And what nationality is **Peter Gordeno**, DM's keyboard player and sometime bassist on stage since 1998?*

A) Italian ☐
B) British ☐
C) Spanish ☐
D) Brazilian ☐

22

*Which of these artists has never released an album with **Mute**?*

A) New Order ☐
B) Einstürzende Neubauten ☐
C) Nick Cave ☐
D) Orchestral Manoeuvres in the Dark ☐
E) Yann Tiersen ☐

23 *On* Remixes 81-04*, the triple CD version released in 2004, which* ***remix artist****, albeit a great fan of the band, did not contribute to one of the 37 tracks on offer?*

A) Goldfrapp ☐
B) Moby ☐
C) William Orbit ☐
D) Timo Maas ☐

24 *Which member or former member of DM takes part in the backing vocals of the song 'Overdrive' on the second album by Client, the electro duo produced by Andy Fletcher?*

A) Dave Gahan ☐
B) Martin Gore ☐
C) Alan Wilder ☐
D) Vince Clarke ☐

25 *In 2010, Martin Gore and Vince Clarke decided to collaborate on a* ***techno record*** *project that would later be named after their respective initials, VCMG. The two friends composed the album entirely remotely and by correspondence. They met up again in May 2011 to finalise the album, which was released on 12 March 2012. Who contacted the other to suggest this project?*

A) Vince contacted Martin ☐
B) Martin contacted Vince ☐

26 *In 2016, Martin Gore contributed vocals to a track by English psychedelic rock band* ***The Mission****, on the album* Another Fall from Grace. *Which track on this album is it?*

A) 'Another Fall from Grace' ☐
B) 'Only You & You Alone' ☐
C) 'Tyranny of Secrets' ☐
D) 'Never's Longer than Forever' ☐

27 *What is the* ***Anglo-American band*** *with whom Dave Gahan has recorded three full-length albums?*

A) MGMT ☐
B) Weezers ☐
C) Soulsavers ☐
D) Kings of Leon ☐

28 *Which U2 song did Depeche Mode cover for* AHK-toong BAY-bi Covered, *the CD of covers released in 2011 to celebrate the 20th anniversary of* **Achtung Baby**?

A) 'Mysterious Ways' ☐
B) 'Zoo Station' ☐
C) 'So Cruel' ☐
D) 'The Fly' ☐

29 *For more than a decade, DM has partnered with a famous watch brand to raise funds for the non-profit organisation "**Charity: Water**", which since 2006 has been working to provide clean drinking water to the world's poorest people. Which brand has DM developed this generous partnership with?*

A) Swatch ☐
B) Rolex ☐
C) Hublot ☐
D) Festina ☐

30 *What is the name of the **Goldfrapp** song that Dave Gahan sings on with Alison Goldfrapp that was released as a single in 2018 by Mute?*

A) 'Melancholy Sky' ☐
B) 'Ocean' ☐
C) 'Everything is Never Enough' ☐
D) 'Anymore' ☐

31 *In 2008, an English band scored a hit with a single that paid tribute to '**Enjoy the Silence**' and the video clip directed by Anton Corbijn, in which Dave Gahan, disguised as a king, drags a folding armchair through grandiose desert landscapes. Who are the band and the single in question?*

A) 'Nude' by Radiohead ☐
B) 'Ulysses' by Franz Ferdinand ☐
C) 'Uprising' by Muse ☐
D) 'Viva la Vida' by Coldplay ☐

32 *Give each artist the title of their **DM cover version**:*

A) Johnny Cash
B) The Smashing Pumpkins
C) Placebo
D) Tori Amos
E) Jimmy Somerville

a) 'Never Let Me Down Again'
b) 'Enjoy the Silence'
c) 'But Not Tonight'
d) 'Personal Jesus'
e) 'I Feel You'

33 *How many **covers** has the band officially released?*

A) 1 ☐
B) 2 ☐
C) 3 ☐
D) 4 ☐

34 *Known all over the world, **DMK** is a Colombian father, Dicken Schrader, and his two children, Milah and Korben. From 2010 to 2022, they recorded covers of DM songs that they broadcast on the Internet in a childish, playful but unstoppably effective way. Here are five tracks and it's up to you to find the one that DMK didn't record and broadcast:*

A) 'Everything Counts' ☐
B) 'The Meaning of Love' ☐
C) 'A Photograph of You' ☐
D) 'Precious' ☐
E) 'Personal Jesus' ☐

35 *Which **Greek synth pop band** released, in cover form, the full-length album* A Broken Frame *in 2015 and the single 'Get the Balance Right' in 2017?*

A) Shamallow ☐
B) Shamarsh ☐
C) Marshmallow ☐
D) Marsheaux ☐

36 *Richard Butler co-wrote the single 'Ghosts Again' with Martin Gore, released in February 2023. This is the first time a track has been co-written with an artist from outside DM. Which **English post-punk band** is R. Butler the leader of?*

A) The Mission ☐
B) Echo & the Bunnymen ☐
C) The Psychedelic Furs ☐
D) Killing Joke ☐

37 *In 2023, **Stella Rose Gahan**, daughter of Dave Gahan and Jennifer Sklias-Gahan born in 1999, released her first album. What's its title?*

A) *Eyes of Stone* ☐
B) *Eyes of Glass* ☐
C) *Heart of Stone* ☐
D) *Heart of Glass* ☐

38 *What is the title of* ***Vince Clarke's first proper solo album****, released by Mute in November 2023?*

A) *Songs of Resilience* ☐
B) *Songs of Absence* ☐
C) *Songs of Silence* ☐
D) *Songs of Innocence* ☐

39 *What is the name of the band for which* ***Dave Gahan*** *sang the two tracks 'Shock Collar' in 2020 and 'Brother' in 2024?*

A) Exit Calm ☐
B) Null + Void ☐
C) Humanist ☐

40 *Three artists have remixed the single '****Wagging Tongue****' for its official numbered limited edition vinyl released on 15 December 2023 under the title* Wagging Tongue (Remixes). *Who didn't work on this track?*

A) Anders Trentemøller ☐
B) Daniel Avery ☐
C) Hawtin Gaiser ☐
D) Hennig Baer ☐

1. C

Robert Smith from The Cure.

2. A

Alison Moyet, born 18 June 1961.

3. D

The Everly Brothers. Bryan Ferry recorded a version on his album *Let's Stick Together* (1976).

4. B

Blancmange.

5. C

On 7 March 1983, Einstürzende Neubauten played their first London concert, supporting The Birthday Party (with another German band, Malaria!) at the Lyceum Ballroom. The Neubauten were also in London in April to record an album at Trident Studios (with Flood, among others) for the Some Bizarre label, with whom they signed a contract in June of that year. It wasn't until 19 August 1983 that Einstürzende Neubauten played their first headline gig in London, at Acklam Hall in Ladbroke Grove. Other sources say that Martin Gore saw Einstürzende Neubauten at the legendary "Concerto For Voice And Machinery" concert at London's Institute of Contemporary Arts (ICA) on 3 January 1984. The concert was interrupted by the staff after twenty-five minutes, because the group was destroying the stage with a jackhammer, and it turned into a riot.

6. B

Recoil.

7. A-c / B-a / C-b

8. B

Modern Girls by Jerry Kramer. 'But Not Tonight' appeared on the soundtrack album, as first track, in its "Robert Margouleff Remix" version (Warner, 1986). This also explains why the song was released as a single on the American market rather than 'Stripped'. [See also question 30 in Part II].

9. D / A / B / C

Bloodline (1991), *Unsound Methods* (1997), *Liquid* (2000), *SubHuman* (2007).

10.

A-d (Joe Crow, lead singer of The Nightingales; the only single under his own name in 1982) / **B-e** (on Tuxedomoon's *Holy Wars* album in 1985) / **C-a** (on The Durutti Column's 3rd album *Another Setting*, 1983) / **D-c** (on the 2nd album *Sleep No More*, 1981, by Sheffield band The Comsat Angels, for whom Composition of Sound supported on 24 September 1980 at the Bridgehouse in Canning Town) / **E-b** (single from The Sparks' 1974 album *Propaganda*).

11. B

It was the English producer Rico Conning who, at the same time, had worked with a number of Mute artists (Laibach, Frank Tovey, Wire).

12. A

The soundtrack was released on 10 December 1991 as *Until The End of the World: Music From the Motion Picture Soundtrack*, with 'Death's Door' as track 13. Apparently only Wilder and Gore worked on it.

13. C

'Coming Back to You'.

14. C

The Cure. Although the request came from Robert Smith himself, it was apparently made indirectly: Perry Bamonte, a member of the Cure at the time, had a brother, Daryl Bamonte, who was at the time co-managing DM's tours, as well as being involved in those of The Cure. Alan Wilder respectfully and politely declined, not wishing to join any other band.

15. E

Simple Minds, although they are a band who have officially released a good number of covers of bands from the same era as the Basildon outfit. See in particular their album *Neon Lights* (2001).

16. D

This is 'A Song for Europe', the third track on the fifteen-track CD.

This is his first official solo recording, here under the name David Gahan, with the full first name, which is rare. Incidentally, the booklet opens with a beautiful photo by Sofia Coppola.

17. C

'World in My Eyes'. Robert Smith confided that he had hesitated between 'World in My Eyes' and 'Walking in My Shoes', but that when he tested both at home, he found that 'World in My Eyes' would be better, given the way he sings. He has made no secret of his admiration for Martin Gore's songs since 1989.

18. B

The title 'Das Lied von einsamen Mädchen' is in German (in English it would be 'The Song of the Lonely Girl'). It's a song popularised by Nico in 1985 on her last album *Camera obscura*, but it's an old German standard written by Robert Gilbert and Werner R. Heymann in 1952. The other ten tracks are sung in English. No instrumentals.

19. C

M. Gore has released five LPs and EPs. Under his own name (Martin L. Gore, with the abbreviated Lee), the two cover albums *Counterfeit e.p.* (1989) and *Counterfeit²* (2003); the instrumental album *MG* (2015) then the EP *The Third Chimpanzee* (2021) under the initials MG. Not forgetting the album *Ssss* with Vince Clarke in 2012, under the name VCMG.

20. A

Christian Eigner is Austrian, born in 1971.

21. B

Peter Gordeno is British and was born in London in 1964.

22. D

Orchestral Manoeuvres in the Dark.

23. B

Moby, who would later remix for DM ('World in my Eyes', for example).

24. B

Martin Gore. 'Overdrive' is the third track on the album *City* (2004), the last one released on Toast Hawaii. [See also questions 38 and 39 in Part I].

25. A

Vince Clarke contacted Martin Gore.

26. B

'Only You & You Alone'.

27. C

Soulsavers, led by Rich Machin and Ian Glover. The three albums are *The Light the Dead See* (2012), *Angels & Ghosts* (2015) and *Imposter* (2021), the last two credited to Dave Gahan & Soulsavers.

28. C

It's 'So Cruel', the 6th track on the CD which contains all twelve tracks from U2's *Achtung Baby* album. *AHK-toong BAY-bi Covered* was released on 25 October 2011, bundled with the December 2011 issue of UK magazine *Q* (No. 305). 'Mysterious Ways' is covered by Snow Patrol, 'Zoo Station' by Nine Inch Nails and 'The Fly' by Gavin Friday.

29. C

Hublot.

30. B

This is 'Ocean', whose version without Gahan is the last track on the *Silver Eye* album (2017) and is, objectively, less rich... The version with Gahan can be found on the deluxe version of the album released a year later (first track on CD 2). It should also be noted that the DM singer appears in the video directed by Alison Goldfrapp herself. The other three tracks are previous Goldfrapp singles.

31. D

'Viva la Vida' by Coldplay. As a teenager, Chris Martin was so impressed by the video that he asked Corbijn to direct the video for their own track, which is packed with nods to the fallen king who roams the world in 'Enjoy the Silence'. ('Uprising' by Muse was not released until 2009).

32.

A-d (2002) / **B-a** (B-side of 1994 single 'Rocket') / **C-e** (on 2000 album *Sleeping with Ghosts*) / **D-b** (on 2001 album *Strange Little Girls*) / **E-c** (on 2004 album *Home Again*).

33. D

Four: 'Route 66' by Bobby Troup (1946), 'Dirt' by The Stooges (on the 1970 album *Fun House*), 'So Cruel' by U2 (on the 1991 album *Achtung Baby*) and 'Heroes' by David Bowie (on the 1977 album of the same name).

34. C

'A Photograph of You' was not one of the tracks DMK released. They now seem to have pulled the plug on the project, but there is still one album that testifies to their talent: *Songs of Tiny Devotion: A Family Tribute to Depeche Mode 2010-2022*, featuring the eleven DM tracks they covered plus one original song ('Pale Blue Dot'). DMK appears in Anton Corbjin's film *Spirits in the Forest – A Depeche Mode Film* [See also Part IV, question 36].

35. D

The Greek female duo is made up of Marianthi Melitsi and Sophie Sarigiannidou. It will not escape anyone that the name Marsheaux comes from the beginning of both their first names.

36. C

The Psychedelic Furs. Going back in time, DM opened for The Psychedelic Furs on 2 June 1981 at London's Hammersmith Palace, then again in Chicago (Aragon Ballroom) on 26 March 1983 during the American leg of the "A Broken Frame Tour".

37. B

Eyes of Glass was released on 19 May 2023 on producer Yves Rothman's KRO Records label. Containing nine tracks, it enabled her group Stella Rose & the Dead Language to support Depeche Mode at Madison Square Garden in New York on 14 April 2023.

38. C

Songs of Silence (it's even Mute's STUMM500 reference, the 500th LP).

39. C

Humanist is a project by English multi-instrumentalist Rob Marshall, who has teamed up with singers such as Mark Lanegan and Joel Cadbury. 'Shock Collar' appeared on the *Humanist* album (2020), while 'Brother' appears on the album *On the Edge of A Lost and Lonely World* (released in July 2024). Humanist supported a number of European concerts on the "Memento Mori World Tour". Exit Calm was Rob Marshall's previous band. As for Null + Void, this is the project of Swiss musician Kurt Uenala, for whom Dave Gahan performed 'Where I Wait' on the *Cryosleep* album in 2017.

40. A

Anders Trentemøller, who once remixed 'Wrong'. Side A features Hawtin Gaiser's remix, while Side AA includes versions by Daniel Avery and Hennig Baer.

What level of Devotee attitude have you achieved?

Before you fill in the table, it's time to collect bonuses! Answer these last three questions and add as many points as you like to your grand total... ☺

1) What is your favourite DM song?

....

2) What is the DM album that you prefer?

....

3) Who is your favourite band member?

....

	Your score	Number of questions
DM In person		50
DM On records		80
DM Visual		40
DM Live		40
DM & Co.		40
Grand total		**250**

Discography: studio albums

1	*Speak & Spell*	October 1981
2	*A Broken Frame*	September 1982
3	*Construction Time Again*	August 1983
4	*Some Great Reward*	September 1984
5	*Black Celebration*	March 1986
6	*Music for the Masses*	September 1987
7	*Violator*	March 1990
8	*Songs of Faith and Devotion*	March 1993
9	*Ultra*	April 1997
10	*Exciter*	May 2001
11	*Playing the Angel*	October 2005
12	*Sounds of the Universe*	April 2009
13	*Delta Machine*	March 2013
14	*Spirit*	March 2017
15	*Memento Mori*	March 2023

Selected bibliography

* Trevor Baker, *Dave Gahan. Depeche Mode & The Second Coming*, Music Press Books, 2009

* Trevor Baker, *Depeche Mode: The Early Years 1981-1993*, Music Press Books, 2013

* Dennis Burmeister & Sascha Lange, *Depeche Mode: Monument. Extended Version*, Blumenbar, 2023 [in German]; English translation of the first German edition: *Depeche Mode : Monument*, Blumenbar, 2013

* Terry Burrows & Daniel Miller, *Mute: A Visual Document from 1978 → Tomorrow*, Thames & Hudson, 2017

* Michael Christopher, *Depeche Mode FAQ: All That's Left To Know About the World's Finest Synth-pop Band*, Backbeat, 2020

* Anton Corbijn, *Depeche Mode by Anton Corbijn*, Taschen, 2021

* Sylvain Fanet, *Depeche Mode*, Le Mot et le Reste, 2023

* Ian Gittins, *Depeche Mode. Faith and Devotion*, Palazzo Editions, 2019

* Martin L. Gore, *Lays. Textes choisis. Édition bilingue. Traduit par Jugurtha Harchaoui*, éditions Normant, 2009

* Stéphanie Lopez, *Depeche Mode: Book of Faith and Devotion*, Naïve, 2014

* Steve Malins, *Depeche Mode. The Biography*, Andre Deutsch Ltd, 1999

* Jonathan Miller, *Stripped: Depeche Mode*, Omnibus Press, 2003

* Sébastien Michaud, *Depeche Mode, Éthique synthétique*, Camion Blanc, 2001 (updated edition 2007)

* Brian J. Robb, *Depeche Mode On Track: Every Album, Every Song*, Sonicbond Publishing, 2023

* Soledad Romero Mariño (text) & Fernando López del Hierro (illustration), *Depeche Mode*, Reservoir Books, 2018 [in Spanish]; English translation: Soledad Romero Mariño & Fernando López del Hierro, *Depeche Mode: The Unauthorized Biography*, Sourcebooks Explore, 2020

* Simon Spence, *Just Can't Get Enough: The Making of Depeche Mode*, Jawbone, 2011

Acknowledgments

Even if I hardly dare, I obviously have to start by thanking Depeche Mode!

Thanks to my Mum, who bought me my first two DM records when I was thirteen in our village supermarket: 45-rpm records of 'Shake the Disease' and 'Master and Servant', in that order, a few weeks apart (yes, you could find all that in a small Centre Leclerc – as it was called then – in Nord-Finistère in those days!); my Mum, who offered me my first DM concert ticket three years later and who, one February evening, drove me and three friends of mine to the concert venue thirty kilometres from home; my Mum, who wrote the cheques I needed to buy the first three singles by mail order from a Parisian import company when I was sixteen...

Thank you to the woman who has been listening to DM with me for over thirty-five years and thank you to our three children, who were almost called Dave, Martin and Andy... (Please forgive me for this bad joke!)

Thanks to Alain, for forty years of DM exchanges, not to mention the rest.
Thanks to all the voluntary and involuntary contributors of ideas and questions.
Thanks to Emma for proof-reading.
Thanks to Stéphane for the layout and suggestions.

Finally, if you spot an error in the facts, reported here as honestly as possible but with no claim to infallibility, please feel free to let me know at this address:
dmquiz250@gmail.com

Imprimé en octobre 2024 dans l'UE
Imprimerie BookPress